100 Hikes in™ Washington's

SOUTH CASCADES and OLYMPICS

Chinook Pass • White Pass • Goat Rocks
Mount St. Helens • Mount Adams

SECOND EDITION

Ira Spring and Harvey Manning

Photos by Bob and Ira Spring

THE
MOUNTAINEERS

09876
7654

Published by The Mountaineers
1001 S.W. Klickitat Way, Suite 201, Seattle, Washington 98134

Published simultaneously in Canada by Douglas & McIntyre, Ltd., 1615 Venables Street, Vancouver, B.C. V5L 2H1

Published simultaneously in Great Britain by Cordee, 3a DeMontfort Street, Leicester, England, LE1 7HD

Manufactured in the United States of America

Edited by Dana Fos
Maps by Helen Sherman
Book layout by Constance Bollen
Cover: Conrad Creek and Gilbert Peak, Goat Rocks Wilderness Area (Hike 27)

Library of Congress Cataloging in Publication Data

Spring, Ira.
    100 hikes in Washington's South Cascades and Olympics : Chinook Pass, White Pass, Goat Rocks, Mount St. Helens, Mount Adams / Ira Spring and Harvey Manning ; photos by Bob and Ira Spring. — 2nd ed.
        p.   cm.
    Rev. ed. of : 100 hikes in the South Cascades and Olympics, ©1985.
    Includes index.
    ISBN 0-89886-301-5
    1. Hiking—Washington (State)—Guide-books.   2. Hiking—Cascade Range—Guide-books.   3. Hiking—Washington (State)—Olympic Mountains—Guide-books.   4. Washington (State)—Description and travel—1981- —Guide-books.   5. Cascade Range—Description and travel—Guide-books.   6. Olympic Mountains (Wash.)—Description and travel—Guide-books.   I. Manning, Harvey.   II. Mountaineers (Society)   III. Spring, Ira.   100 hikes in the South Cascades and Olympics.   IV. Title.   V. Title: One hundred hikes in Washington's South Cascades and Olympics.
GV199.42.W2S66   1992
917.97'0443—dc20   91-40979
                                                            CIP

CONTENTS

Location   *Status*

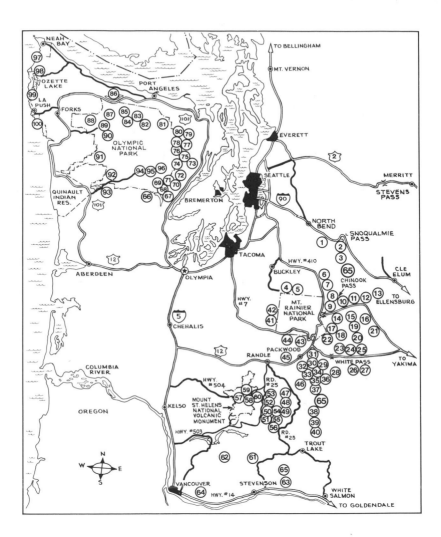

6

Location		Status
		Colonel Bob Wilderness
Pacific Ocean		Olympic National Park

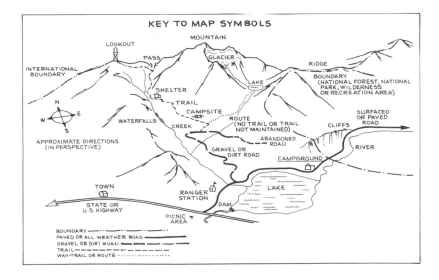

A permit system is being considered in all wilderness areas in the State of Washington. Starting in 1993, permits will be required in the Goat Rocks, Mount Adams, Indian Heaven, Tatoosh, Glacier View, and Trapper Wilderness. In 1994 the William O. Douglas Wilderness will be added to the list.

During 1993, 1994, and 1995 the Forest Service plans to make the permits available at each trailhead. Afterward, hikers should check with the Forest Service before starting out.

Nelson Ridge (Hike 19) from American Ridge (Hike 15)

INTRODUCTION

The country sampled by these 100 hikes has many characteristics in common throughout, and in common, too, with companion volumes on the region north of Snoqualmie Pass. There are, however, significant differences from place to place caused by variations in climate, geology, elevation, and the amount and sort of human use. The Olympic Mountains have an "ocean side"—the west side and south slopes where storms from the Pacific wash ashore like so many giant waves on a beach—and a "rainshadow side"—the relatively arid north and east where the clouds are mainly empties. The two merge in the middle of the range, a spacious wilderness of glaciers and crags and flower fields, rainforests and subalpine parklands and alpine tundras, and one of the largest wildlife populations in America.

The Cascade Range south from Snoqualmie Pass to Norse Peak Wilderness is a checkerboard of private and public tree farms more densely inhabited by logging trucks than hikers, who find few attractions except the Pacific Crest National Scenic Trail, leading from one scenic clearcut to another.

As Rainier, set off west of the crest, rises higher and sprawls wider in the eye of the south-walking traveler, the main line of the range thrusts up the craggy peaks and bright meadows of the Norse Peak Wilderness. Where this unit ends, at Chinook Pass, the William O. Douglas Wilderness begins, extending south to White Pass, the hiker's view west to storm-wet, rain-green, ice-white Mount Rainier National Park, and east to steppes of Central Washington, where sunshine-country and snow-country plants blossom side by side.

From White Pass south the story is all volcanoes: the ancient, deep-dissected ruins of a fire mountain once perhaps on the scale of Adams, in the Goat Rocks Wilderness; Adams, outbulked only by Rainier, in the Mount Adams Wilderness; a landscape spattered with cinder cones and covered by lava flows, some eroded and forested, as in the Trapper Wilderness, others high and meadowed, as in the Indian Heaven Wilderness; and never to be ignored, not even before 1980, the centerpiece of the Mount St. Helens National Volcanic Monument.

The hiking season in low-elevation valleys of the Olympics—and on the zero-elevation beaches—is the whole year; higher, the flowers may not poke through snowbanks until late July, a mere several weeks before their frozen seeds are blanketed by the new winter's white; higher still, there are no flowers ever, and no real hiking season either, only a climbing season. There are places on the east of the Cascades where on any day of the year a person has an 85 percent chance of getting a sunburn, and others, on the west slope of the Olympics, where on any day of the year a person has an 85 percent chance of getting soaking wet right through his rubber boots and rainproof parka, and others, as on the Cascade Crest, where hikers within a mile of each other are at one and the same time gasping from thirst (east) and sputtering like a whale (west).

Administration

Mount Rainier and Olympic National Parks have been set aside, to use the words of the National Park Act of 1916, "to conserve the scenery and the natural and historic objects and wildlife...." Each visitor must therefore enjoy the parks "in such manner and by such means as will leave them unimpaired for the enjoyment of future generations." A good motto for park users is: "Take only a picture, leave only a footprint." Motorized (and mechanized, including "mountain bikes") travel on park trails is forbidden and horse travel closely regulated. Hunting is banned—but not fishing. Pets are not allowed on trails, because their presence disturbs wildlife.

Backcountry permits are required for all overnight hikers in national parks and may be obtained at ranger stations on the entry roads.

Under U.S. Forest Service jurisdiction in the South Cascades are the Goat Rocks, Mount Adams, Clearwater, Glacier View, Tatoosh, Trapper Creek, Indian Heaven, William O. Douglas, and Norse Peak Wildernesses, and in the Olympics, the Wonder Mountain, Mount Skokomish, The Brothers, Buckhorn, and Colonel Bob Wildernesses, where "the earth and its community of life are untrammeled by man, where man himself is a visitor who does not remain." Motorized (and mechanized) travel is forbidden absolutely and horse travel is beginning to be regulated or at some places even eliminated; foot travel and camping are currently less restricted, though the backcountry population explosion will require increasing controls to protect the fragile ecosystems.

Also under the Forest Service is the Mount St. Helens National Volcanic Monument, where management plans are still evolving, one wary ear always cocked to hear what more the volcano may have to say on the subject.

Maps

The sketch maps in this book are intended to give only a general idea of the terrain and trails. Once out of the city and off the highways, the navigation demands precision.

The U.S. Forest Service system of road numbers gives main roads two numerals. For example, the Randle to Trout Lake road is No. 23 and is show on Forest Service maps as 23 and described in the guidebook as road No. 23. Secondary roads have the first two numerals of the main road plus two additional numerals. For example, from road No. 23 the secondary road to Killen Creek trailhead is numbered 2329 and shown on the forest map as 2329 . Three more numerals are added for a spur road, so a spur from road No. 2329 to Takhlakh Lake becomes road No. 2329026. It is shown as 026 on road signs and 026 on Forest Service road maps. In this guidebook the road is described as (2329)026.

A veteran traveler of the South Cascades, relying on his faithful file of well-worn Forest Service maps, had best never leave civilization without a full tank of gas, survival rations, and instructions to family or friends on when to call out the Logging Road Search and Rescue Team. A party would do better to obtain the current National Forest recreational maps, which are cumbersome for the trail but essential to get about on the renumbered roads. These maps may be obtained for a small fee at ranger stations or by writing Forest Supervisors at:

Mt. Baker–Snoqualmie
 National Forest
21905 64th Ave. West
Mountlake Terrace, WA 98043

Gifford Pinchot National Forest
6926 East Fourth Plain Blvd.
P.O. Box 8944
Vancouver, WA 98668-8944

Wenatchee National Forest
P.O. Box 811
Wenatchee, WA 98801

Olympic National Forest
Federal Building
Olympia, WA 98501

Also available from ranger stations, as well as from map shops and sporting goods stores, are the Forest Service maps for Goat Rocks, Mount Adams, William O. Douglas, Tatoosh–Glacier View, and Indian Heaven–Trapper Creek Wildernesses, excellent for hikers.

The best maps in the history of the world are the topographic sheets produced by the U.S. Geological Survey (USGS), and these, too, are sold by map shops and sporting goods stores. However, revision is so occasional that information on roads and trails is always largely obsolete. Essential as they are for off-trail, cross-country explorers, in this book we have recommended them only when there is no alternative.

As it happens, among the merits of the USGS is that it sells the data "separations" (from which its sheets are published) on a nonprofit, cost-only, public-service basis. This has enabled commercial publishers to buy the separations, add and delete information, and issue maps that are designed specifically for hikers and are kept up to date. Though the USGS base map is always available, for areas where they exist we recommend the maps in the Green Trails series, which covers virtually all hiking areas in the Cascades and Olympics, and the Custom Correct series for the Olympics.

Clothing and Equipment

Many trails described in this book can be walked easily and safely, at least along the lower portions, by any person capable of getting out of a car and onto his feet, and without any special equipment whatever.

To such people we can only say, "welcome to walking—but beware!" Northwest mountain weather, especially on the ocean side of the ranges, is notoriously undependable. Cloudless morning skies can be followed by afternoon deluges of rain or fierce squalls of snow. Even without a storm a person can get mighty chilly on high ridges when—as often happens—a cold wind blows under a bright sun and pure blue sky.

No one should set out on a Cascade or Olympic trail, unless for a brief stroll, lacking warm long pants, a wool (or the equivalent) shirt or sweater, and a windproof and rain-repellent parka, coat, or poncho. And on the feet—sturdy shoes or boots plus two pairs of wool socks and an extra pair in the rucksack.

As for that rucksack, it should also contain the Ten Essentials, found to be so by generations of members of The Mountaineers, often from sad experience:

1. Extra clothing—more than needed in good weather.
2. Extra food—enough so something is left over at the end of the trip.
3. Sunglasses—necessary for most alpine travel and indispensable on snow.
4. Knife—for first aid and emergency firebuilding (making kindling).
5. Firestarter—a candle or chemical fuel for starting a fire with wet wood.
6. First aid kit.
7. Matches—in a waterproof container.
8. Flashlight—with extra bulb and batteries.
9. Map—be sure it's the right one for the trip.
10. Compass—be sure to know the declination, east or west.

Management

In recent decades hikers have enjoyed spectacular successes in the halls of Congress and the corridors of federal bureaucracies, preserving many miles of threatened trails, here and there even recovering trails that had been sacrificed to wheels. Now we find ourselves in danger of losing much of what we have fought for—losing it by loving it. Feet are doing it, human feet by the millions. Hooves, too, of horses, mules, donkeys, and llamas, far fewer in number but doing grossly disproportionate damage. Their (and our) calls of nature, and our garbage, our fires, and our tents and sleeping bags are doing a dirty job.

The following sections summarize the principles of caring wildland behavior. The formal, official regulations vary from one jurisdiction to another, depending on the vulnerability of the terrain, the volume of travel, and perceptions of the individual managers. The responsibility of the hiker is to inform himself about the regulations of each trail he walks and to observe them—not because a wilderness ranger may come by and issue a citation, but because it's the right thing to do, and because Old Coyote is watching over us all and may come in the night and give bad hikers very bad dreams.

Camping and Fires

Indiscriminate camping blights alpine meadows. A single small party may trample grass, flowers, and heather so badly that they don't recover from the shock for several years. If the same spot is used several or more times a summer, year after year, the greenery vanishes, replaced by bare dirt. The respectful traveler always aims to camp in the woods or in rocky morainal areas. These alternatives lacking, it is better to use a meadow site already bare—in technical terminology, "hardened"—rather than extend the destruction into virginal places nearby.

Particularly to be avoided are camps on soft meadows (hard rock or bare-dirt site may be quite all right) on the banks of streams and lakes. Delightful and scenic as such sites are, their use may endanger the water purity, as well as the health of delicate plants. Moreover, a camp on a viewpoint makes the beauty unavailable to other hikers who want to simply come and look, or eat lunch, and then go camp in the woods.

Carry a collapsible water container to minimize the trips to the water supply that beat down a path. (As a bonus, the container lets you camp high on a dry ridge, where the solitude and the views are.)

Carry a lightweight pair of camp shoes, less destructive to plants and soils than trail boots.

As the age of *laissez-faire* camping yields to the era of thoughtful management, different policies are being adopted in different places. For example, high-use spots may be designated "Day Use Only," forbidding camps. In others there is a blanket rule against camps within 100 feet of the water. However, in certain areas rangers have inventoried existing camps, found 95 percent are within 100 feet of the water, and decided it is better to keep existing sites, where the vegetation has long since disappeared, than to establish new "barrens" elsewhere. The rule in such places is "use established sites"; wilderness rangers on their rounds disestablish those sites judged unacceptable.

Be careful to avoid pitching your tarp or tent in a potential flood zone. Ditching will ruin vegetation, so unless the ground is already bare, never ditch the sleeping area.

Always carry a sleeping pad of some sort to keep your bag dry and your bones comfortable. Do not revert to the ancient bough bed of the frontier past.

Always seek to camp invisibly—that is, well away from the trail, where your presence will not intrude on the sense of wildland isolation sought by others.

The wood fire is virtually obsolete in the high country. At best, dry firewood is hard to find at popular camps. What's left, the picturesque silver snags and logs, is part of the scenery, too valuable to be wasted cooking a pot of soup. It should be needless to say that green, living wood must never be cut; it doesn't burn anyway.

For reasons of both convenience and conservation, the highland hiker should carry a lightweight stove for cooking (or not cook—though the food is cold, the inner man is hot) and depend on clothing and shelter (and sunset strolls) for evening warmth. The pleasures of a roaring blaze on a cold mountain night are indisputable, but a single party on a single night may use up ingredients of the scenery that were long decades in growing, dying, and silvering.

In forests, fires perhaps may still be built with a clear conscience. Again, one should minimize impact by using only established fire pits and using only dead and down wood. When finished, be certain the fire is absolutely out—drown the coals and stir them with a stick and then drown the ashes until the smoking and steaming have stopped completely and a finger stuck in the slurry feels no heat. Embers can smoulder underground in dry duff for days, spreading gradually and days later starting a forest fire.

If you decide to build a fire, do not make a new fire ring—use an existing one. In popular areas patrolled by rangers, its existence means this is an approved, "established" or "designated," campsite. If a fire ring has been heaped over with rocks, it means the site has been disestablished.

Fires may be said to be coming down the mountain, year by year; they are banned absolutely in most meadowlands; in some jurisdictions they are not allowed above a certain elevation, perhaps 3500 feet. Moreover, no longer is sea level a free-fire zone. The olden-day bonfire is *out:* On the Olympic Park Coastal Strip, fires must be no closer than 10 feet to driftwood logs and may not exceed 3 feet in diameter.

Litter and Garbage and Sanitation

The rule among considerate hikers is: *If you can carry it in full, you can carry it out empty.* Don't leave it for some backcountry ranger to pack it out for you.

On a day hike, take back to the road (and garbage can) every last orange peel and gum wrapper.

On an overnight or longer hike, burn all paper (if a fire is built) but carry back all unburnables, including cans, metal foil, plastic, glass, and papers that won't burn.

Don't bury garbage. If fresh, animals will dig it up and scatter the remnants. Burning before burying is no answer either. Tin cans take as long as 40 years to disintegrate completely; aluminum and glass last for centuries. Furthermore, digging pits to bury junk disturbs the ground cover.

Don't leave leftover food for the next travelers; they will have their own supplies and won't be tempted by "gifts" spoiled by time or chewed by animals.

Especially don't cache plastic tarps. Weathering quickly ruins the fabric, little creatures nibble, and the result is a useless, miserable mess.

Keep the water pure. Don't wash dishes in streams or lakes, loosing food particles and detergent. Haul buckets of water to the woods or rocks,

Greenwater valley (Hike 6)

and wash and rinse there. Don't wash bodies in streams or lakes. Don't swim in waters being taken internally by others. Eliminate body waste in places well removed from watercourses; first dig a shallow hole in the "biological disposer layer," then touch a match to the toilet paper (or better, use leaves), and finally cover the evidence. So managed, the wastes are consumed in a matter of days. Where privies are provided, use them.

Party Size

One management technique used to minimize impact in popular areas is to limit the number of people in any one group to a dozen or fewer. Hikers with very large families (or outing groups from clubs or whatever) should check the rules when planning a trip.

Pets

The handwriting is on the wall for dog-owners. Pets always have been forbidden on national park trails, and now some parts of wildernesses are being closed to them. How fast the ban spreads will depend on the owners' sensitivity, training, acceptance of responsibility, and courtesy—and on the expressed wishes of nonowners.

Where pets are permitted, even a well-behaved dog can ruin a stranger's trip. Some dogs noisily defend an ill-defined territory for their master, "guard" him on the trail, snitch enemy bacon, and are quite likely to defecate on the flat bit of ground the next hiker will want to sleep on.

For a long time to come, there will be plenty of "empty" country for those who hunt upland game with dogs or who simply can't enjoy a family outing without ol' Rover. However, the family that wants to go where the crowds are must leave its best friend home.

Do not depend on tolerance of wilderness neighbors. Some people are so harassed at home by loose dogs that a hound in the wilderness has the same effect on them as a motorcycle. They may holler at you and turn you in to the ranger.

Dogs belong to the same family as coyotes, and even if no wildlife is visible, a dog's presence is sensed by the small wild things into whose home it is intruding.

Water

Hikers traditionally have drunk the water in wilderness in confidence, doing their utmost to avoid contaminating it so the next person also can safely drink. But there is no assurance your predecessor was so careful.

Nowadays, no open water ever can be considered certainly safe for human consumption. Any reference in this book to "drinking water" is not a guarantee. It is entirely up to the individual to judge the situation and decide whether to take a chance.

In the late 1970s began a great epidemic of giardiasis, caused by a parasite that spends part of its life cycle swimming free in water, and part in the intestinal tract of beavers and other wildlife, dogs, and people. Actually, the "epidemic" was solely in the press; _Giardia_ were first identified in the eighteenth century and are present in the public water system of many cities of the world and many towns in America—including some in the foothills of the Cascades. Long before the "outbreak" of "beaver fever," there was the well-known malady, the "Boy Scout trots." This is not to make light of the disease; though most humans feel no ill effects (but many become carriers), others have serious symptoms, which include devastating diarrhea, and the treatment is nearly as unpleasant. The reason giardiasis has become "epidemic" is that there are more people in the backcountry—more people drinking water contaminated by animals—and more people contaminating the water.

Whenever in doubt, boil the water 10 minutes. Keep in mind that *Giardia* can survive in water at or near freezing for weeks or months—a snow pond is not necessarily safe. Boiling is 100 percent effective against not only *Giardia* but the myriad of other filthy little blighters that may upset your digestion or—as with some forms of hepatitis—destroy your liver.

If you cannot boil, use one of the several *iodine* treatments (chlorine compounds have been found untrustworthy in wildland circumstances), such as Potable Aqua or the more complicated method that employs iodine crystals. Rumors to the contrary, iodine treatments pose no threat to the health.

Be *wary* of the filters sold in backpacking shops. One or two have been tested and are thought to be probably reliable (not against hepatitis) and new products are coming on the market but the rule must be *caveat emptor*—would you bet your liver on the promise of an advertising agency?

Horses

Most horse-riders (and llama-leaders) do their best to be good neighbors on the trail and know how to go about it. The typical hiker, though, is ignorant of the difficulties in maneuvering a huge mass of flesh (containing a very small brain) along narrow paths on steep mountains.

The first rule is the horse has the right of way. For his own safety as well as that of the rider, the hiker must get off the trail—preferably on the downhill side, giving the clumsy animal and its perilously perched rider the inside of the tread. If necessary—as, say, on the Goat Rocks Crest—retreat some distance to a safe passing point.

The second rule is, when you see the horse approaching, do not keep silent or stand still in a mistaken attempt to avoid frightening the beast. Continue normal motions and speak to it, so the creature will recognize you as just another human and not think you a silent and doubtless dangerous monster.

Finally, if you have a dog along, get a tight grip on its throat to stop the nipping and yapping, which may endanger the rider and, in the case of a surly horse, the dog as well.

Most horse-riders are considerate campers, abstaining from using camps to unload and load, in the process scattering manure, which attracts flies and mice. However, horsemen who claim frontiersman privileges are undergoing a difficult period of re-education. Hikers should not try to be policemen but should report inappropriate actions when they see them.

Theft

A quarter-century ago theft from a car left at the trailhead was rare. Not now. Equipment has become so fancy and expensive and hikers so numerous, that stealing is a high-profit industry. Not even wilderness camps are entirely safe, but the professionals mainly concentrate on cars.

Rangers have the following recommendations.

First and foremost, don't make crime profitable for the pros. If they break into a hundred cars and get nothing but moldy boots and tattered T-shirts they'll give up. Don't think locks help—pros can open your car door and trunk as fast with a picklock as you can with your key. Don't imagine you can hide anything from them—they know all the hiding spots. If the hike is part of an extended car trip, arrange to store your extra equipment at a nearby motel.

Be suspicious of anyone waiting at a trailhead. One of the tricks of the trade is to sit there with a pack as if waiting for a ride, watching new arrivals unpack—and hide their valuables—and maybe even striking up a conversation to determine how long the marks will be away.

The ultimate solution, of course, is for hikers to become as poor as they were in the olden days. No criminal would consider trailheads profitable if the loot consisted solely of shabby khaki war surplus.

Safety Considerations

The reason the Ten Essentials are advised is that hiking in the backcountry entails unavoidable risk that every hiker assumes and must be aware of and respect. The fact that a trail is described in this book is not a representation that it will be safe for you. Trails vary greatly in difficulty and in the degree of conditioning and agility one needs to enjoy them safely. On some hikes routes may have changed or conditions may have deteriorated since the descriptions were written. Also, trail conditions can change even from day to day, owing to weather and other factors. A trail that is safe on a dry day or for a highly conditioned, agile, properly equipped hiker may be completely unsafe for someone else or unsafe under adverse weather conditions.

You can minimize your risks on the trail by being knowledgeable, prepared, and alert. There is not space in this book for a general treatise on safety in the mountains, but there are a number of good books and public courses on the subject and you should take advantage of them to increase your knowledge. Just as important, you should always be aware of your own limitations and of conditions existing when and where you are hiking. If conditions are dangerous, or if you are not prepared to deal with them safely, choose a different hike! It's better to have a wasted drive than to be the subject of a mountain rescue.

These warnings are not intended to scare you off the trails. Hundreds of thousands of people have safe and enjoyable hikes every year. However, one element of the beauty, freedom, and excitement of the wilderness is the presence of risks that do not confront us at home. When you hike you assume those risks. They can be met safely, but only if you exercise your own independent judgment and common sense.

To help hikers have a safe and enjoyable trail experience matching the trip to experience and physical condition, the Forest Service has begun signing trails as follows:

Requires limited skill and has little physical challenge. Tread is smooth, level, and wide, with generous clearing of trees, limbs, and other vegetation above and to each side of the trail to permit easy passage. Elevation gain or loss is minimal. Streams are most often crossed with bridges.

Requires a moderate skill level and provides a moderate physical challenge. Tread surface contains roots and embedded rocks. Clearing of trees, limbs, and other vegetation above and to each side of the trail results in occasional contact by the users. Elevation gain or loss is moderate. Streams are most often crossed by fords.

Requires a high degree of skill and provides a lot of physical challenge. Tread is seldom graded except on steep slopes for safety and prevention of soil erosion. Minimal clearing of trees, limbs, and other vegetation results in hampering the progress of the user. Elevation gain or loss is usually severe. Streams are crossed by fording and are sometimes difficult.

Protect This Land, Your Land

The Cascades and Olympic country is large and rugged and wild—but it is also, and particularly in the scenic climaxes favored by hikers, a fragile country. If man is to blend into the ecosystem, rather than dominate and destroy, he must walk lightly, respectfully, always striving to make his passage through the wilderness invisible.

The public servants entrusted with administration of the region have a complex and difficult job, and they desperately need the cooperation of every wildland traveler. Here, the authors would like to express appreciation to these dedicated men and women for their advice on what trips to include in this book and for their detailed review of the text and maps. Thanks are due the Superintendent of Olympic National Park, the Supervisors of the Wenatchee, Gifford Pinchot, and Olympic National Forests, and their district rangers and other staff members.

On behalf of the U.S. Forest Service and National Park Service and The Mountaineers, we invite Americans—and all citizens of Earth—to come and see and live in their Washington Cascades and Olympics and, while enjoying some of the world's finest wildlands, to vow henceforth to share in the task of preserving the trails and ridges, lakes and rivers, forests and flower gardens for future generations, our children and grandchildren, who will need the wilderness experience at least as much as we do, and probably more.

Seven Lakes Basin from Bogachiel Peak (Hike 87)

SAVING OUR TRAILS

Preservation Goals for the 1990s and Beyond

In the early 1960s, The Mountaineers began publishing trail guides as another means of working "to preserve the natural beauty of Northwest America," through putting more feet on certain trails, in certain wildlands. We suffered no delusion that large numbers of boots improve trails or enhance wildness. However, we had learned to our rue that "you use it or lose it," that threatened areas could only be saved if they were more widely known and treasured. We were criticized in certain quarters for contributing to the deterioration of wilderness by publicizing it, and confessed the fault, but could only respond, "Which would you prefer: A hundred boots in a virgin forest? Or that many snarling wheels in a clearcut?"

As the numbers of wilderness lovers have grown so large as to endanger the qualities they love, the rules of "walking light" and "camping no trace" must be more faithfully observed. Yet the ultimate menace to natural beauty is not hikers, no matter how destructive their great vicious boots may be, nor even how polluting their millions of *Giardia* cysts are, but doomsday, arriving on two or three or four or six or eight wheels, or on tractor treads, or on whirling wings—the total conquest of the land and water and sky by machinery.

Victories Past

Conceived in campfire conversation of the 1880s, Olympic National Park was established in 1938, the grandest accomplishment of our most conservation-minded president, Franklin D. Roosevelt. (Confined to a wheelchair and never himself able to know the trails with his own feet, FDR nevertheless saw the fallacy in the sneering definition of wilderness as "preserves for the aristocracy of the physically fit" and knew the value of dreams that never could be personally attained.)

A renewal of the campaigns after World War II brought—regionally, in 1960—the Glacier Peak Wilderness and—nationally, in 1964—the Wilderness Act, whereby existing and future wildernesses were placed beyond the fickleness of bureaucracies, guarded by Congress and the president against officious tampering.

The year 1968 saw the North Cascades Act, achieving another vision of the nineteenth century, the North Cascades National Park, plus the Lake Chelan and Ross Lake National Recreation Areas, Pasayten Wilderness, and additions to the Glacier Peak Wilderness.

In 1976 the legions of citizens laboring at the grass roots, aided by the matching dedication of certain of their congressmen and senators, obtained the Alpine Lakes Wilderness. In 1984 the same alliance, working at the top and at the bottom and all through the middle, all across the state, won the Washington Wilderness Act encompassing more than 1,000,000 acres, including in the purview of this volume these new wildernesses—Clearwater, Norse Peak, William O. Douglas, Glacier View, Tatoosh, Indian Heaven, Trapper Creek, Wonder Mountain, Mount Skokomish, The Brothers, Buckhorn, and Colonel Bob—and additions to Goat Rocks and Mount Adams.

Is, therefore, the job done?

Goals Ahead

Absolutely not.

Had hikers been content with the victory of 1938, there never would have been those of 1960, 1968, 1976, and 1984. The American nation as a whole has a step or two yet to go before attaining that condition of flawless perfection where it fits seamlessly into the final mosaic of the Infinite Plan, and the same is true of the National Wilderness Preservation System.

However, it needs to be kept uppermost in mind that designation as "wilderness" or "national park" or "national monument" is a means, not the end. The goals ahead are not words on a document or lines on a map but the protection of land these symbols may signify. Any other symbols that do the job are satisfactory. The *protection* is the thing.

In contrast to the immediate past, the preservationist agenda of the immediate future is focused less on redrawing maps than employing any practical method available to preserve roadless areas from further invasion by machinery. In fact, we are now at a stage where the saving of trails, important though that is, has a lower priority than the saving of fisheries and wildlife resources, scientific values, gene pools, and another contribution of wildland too long neglected, the provision of dependable and pure water for domestic and agricultural needs.

Setting aside the Greenhouse Effect, the hole in the ozone layer, and the steady draining away of the resources of civilization into fruitless wars, the highest Washington priority in the wildland department of human concerns is the preservation of "ancient forests," the more precise term newly adopted to replace "old-growth." With 90 percent of the original forest cover of the state already logged, it should be self-evident that the remaining 10 percent could not put off more than several years the necessity to reform the forest industry for the long-run future. Facing up to reality is exceedingly difficult in a community where that reality requires hundreds of families to radically alter their way of life. However, the trauma is inevitable, the only question being whether it takes place in the early 1990s or later. Fortunately, the nation has become alarmed and enraged at the way a *national* resource, a *national* treasure, is being destroyed for purely local and very short-run benefit.

The technicalities of the status of the ancient forests—whether they are placed in park, wilderness, ecological preserves, wildlife refuges, or whatever categories may be devised—are the second step of an action program. The first is to save these forest ecosystems, which, once logged, cannot be reconstituted in pristine condition for many, many centuries, if not millennia.

Meanwhile, the flood of humanity hungering for wilderness is forcing us to restructure our preservation strategies. This is *not* to propose a revision of the Wilderness Act of 1960—that charter must be held intact, every attempt at amendment repulsed, because though wilderness-management principles of the 1950s may not be in every respect perfectly suited to the 1990s, to open the door a crack for minor adjustments would let in a howling horde demanding that the wilderness be "opened up to the people"—meaning the people in helicopters, on bicycles, carrying portable spas and electricity generators and Coke machines.

The wilderness cores must be kept pristine. The focus of rethinking should be the wilderness edges. Even here, care must be taken not to degrade those areas adjoining existing wildernesses, which ultimately must be added to the preserves; the Glacier Peak Wilderness proposed in the 1950s was only partially granted by the Forest Service in 1960, two subsequent actions by Congress have gained the most minimal enlargements, and preservationists never will rest until the original vision is fulfilled in total.

Still, if there could be wilderness-edge areas that enjoyed wilderness-type exclusions of roads and mechanized equipment yet provided more extensive and higher-grade trail systems than are proper in the wilderness cores, plus privies to prevent contamination of the precious liquid essence of the wild earth, and perhaps "hardened" tent sites and the like, larger numbers of hikers could be accommodated; protecting the pristinity of the core ecosystems by rationing would be much more acceptable if such nonrationed alternatives were available.

Following are several classifications currently in use, or proposed.

Roadless Areas

Current plans of national forests delineate a number of "roadless areas" that temporarily reprieve from road-building most of the non-wilderness trails in this guidebook. However, unless Congress takes action to provide permanent protection, the Forest Service can change its mind tomorrow and replace the trails with logging roads.

Reconstituted Roadless Area

In the eastern United States, the National Wilderness System is being augmented by New Wildernesses. The concept could play an important role in Washington. For example, in the Cascades and Olympics outside the dedicated parks and wildernesses, there are highlands skinned by "timber miners" at elevations where a second crop of commercial trees will not grow for 500 years or more, far too long for credible tree-farming. Within decades, however, the land will green up in scrub and shrubs, streams will restabilize, and wildlife populations come into balance. Old logging roads can be allowed to dwindle to footpaths. Old "landings" where logs were loaded on railroad cars or trucks can become campsites where backpackers can look out at night to the lights of farms and cities—and by turning, look *inward* to starlit wilderness cores.

A complete system of protected trail country in Washington might well include such "reconstituted roadless areas" as "wilderness-edge backcountry."

Regional Wilderness

"Regional wildernesses" are defined by the East San Francisco Bay Regional Park District as preserves of 2500 acres or more where the evidences of human development are being or can be obliterated by the passage of time and where the terrain is such that sights and sounds of surrounding civilization are substantially muted. On the west edge of the Cascades, four candidate examples may be cited: the Mount Si Natural Resources Conservation Area and the West Tiger Mountain NRCA, managed by the state Department of Natural Resources; Squak Mountain State Park, managed by Washington State Parks; and the Cougar Mountain Regional Wildland Park, managed by King County Parks. Situated a half-hour's drive or less from the homes of millions of people,

these wildland trails provide a wealth of hiking mere minutes from the back door, removing much pressure from the National Wilderness that the folks of Seattle and Yakima must share with the folks of San Diego and Hoboken. In the companion series to this book, the three volumes of *Footsore: Walks and Hikes around Puget Sound* describe hundreds of in-city and near-city trails, introductions to "the wildness within."

What in the World Happened to Us?

The wheel is more than the symbol. It is the fact. The National Wilderness Act so recognizes by banning "mechanical travel," including *but not limited to* motorized travel; bicycles—"mountain bikes"—are excluded too, for the simple reason that in appropriate terrain they readily can go 5–15 miles per hour, an "unnatural" speed incompatible with the natural 1–3 miles per hour of the traveler on foot.

Outside the boundaries of dedicated wilderness, some existing hiker-horse routes, such as abandoned logging roads, can be amicably opened to bicycles, even though the routes then cease being *true trails,* having become *bikeways,* which are a species of *road.* Nevertheless, a route wide enough and with light enough traffic can accommodate bicycles and pedestrians, both capable of being quiet and minimally destructive and disruptive of the backcountry scene. Attach a motor to the wheel, however, and the route not only no longer deserves to be called a "trail," it becomes a *motor road,* closer kin to an interstate freeway.

In this past quarter-century, the concerted efforts of tens of thousands of conservationists have protected large expanses of wildland from invasion by machines—but during the same period, a comparative handful of ORVers have taken away more miles of trail, converting them to *de facto* roads, than the conservationists have saved. As the score stood in 1985, 45 percent of Washington trails were machine-free by being in national parks and wildernesses; of the other 55 percent, half were open to motorcycles—and thus were not truly trails at all. The situation in 1993 is very little better—and in large part, due to the abrupt invasion of the "mountain bike," far worse.

"Getting Along"

Nobody likes a hog. Everybody agrees that nice people unselfishly share the good things the Earth has given us in common. They are tolerant of the fun and foibles of other folks. They do their best to "get along."

Hikers (and their companions of many generations, the horse-riders), have been under steady attack, ever since the end of World War II, as wilderness hogs, trying to keep all that great backcountry for their selfish fun, denying others their equal rights under the Declaration of Independence and the Constitution.

When the sainted Gifford Pinchot announced that national forests were to be managed "for the greatest good of the greatest number in the

Goat Creek and Mount Adams (Hike 34)

long run," he set his U.S. Forest Service on a course of philosophical confusion that, if not cleared up, inevitably will lead to the agency's self-destruction. The Pinchot dogma, restated as "multiple-use," never has been informed by the insights of ecology or social ethics. Each new demand on the wildland of the national forests has been greeted with open arms, treated as equal to every other of the older utilizations. No evaluation is made of the stresses placed on the land nor the disruption of established uses. In the Realm of Pinchot, everybody is equal. Of course, as in Orwell's *Animal Farm,* some are more equal than others. When two modes of travel meet on the trail, the bigger drives out the smaller, the noisier the quieter, the faster the slower, the more costly the less costly. That's not justice. That's simply the way it is.

The war-surplus jeep of World War II drove hikers off the historic route of the emigrant trail over Naches Pass, the Middle Fork Snoqualmie River from Taylor River to Goldmeyer Hot Springs, and a few hundred other old favorites. Then came the motorbike, invented in Washington but refined and mass-produced in Japan, and, in its wake, the ATV and the ORV. Recently a California invention, the "mountain bike," has arrived in Washington (and has spread across the nation), and though it has the potential to be as quiet as a hiker (if only the "bombers" didn't have to giggle, yip, and scream curses at wheel-less travelers who obstruct the way) it has been expelling hikers who come for a relaxed and peaceful, not a kinetic and combative, day. What next? New on the scene is the kiddy's scooter with wide tread for off-pavement travel, light enough to carry uphill for a whizz-bang downhill scoot, and the off-pavement, (trail) rollerskate. After that, the all-terrain pogo stick?

The spirit of Pinchot may be trusted to gaze benignly down on every new arrival and chide hikers to "get along with others."

Not to tar all the national forests with the same brush, Mt. Baker–Snoqualmie, which on occasion has been blessed in the past by supervisors of vision, has attempted to separate conflicting uses so that each, on its own ground, can get along with itself. However, the other Forest Service supervisors consistently have turned a blind eye to what they condescendingly term "perceived conflict," meaning *they* don't see a problem, not in their headquarters offices; their policy is to let the users fight it out on the trails.

Still, when in the course of the lengthy process of forest planning they were required by law to solicit public comment, and found themselves deluged by hiker protests, they conceded that the conflict, existent or imaginary, did indeed appear to be rather widely perceived. Okanogan and Wenatchee National Forests, longtime zealots of jeeps and dirtbikes and every other manifestation of Progress, grudgingly returned a few trails to hikers. Gifford Pinchot National Forest tried a different approach, forming a task force of trail-users who gathered to resolve conflicts by separating the uses. Compromises were forced on both sides; some conflicts were resolved (at least to the satisfaction of the task force) with surprising ease, but hikers had to literally buy back other trails. That is, a mile of new ORV trail must be built before a mile of old trail is returned to hikers. Forest Service money normally spent on improving hiker/horse trails will be diverted to ORVs.

Klickitat Trail and Smith Creek valley from Cispus Butte (Hike 46)

In the experience of the authors of this book, most Forest Service officers are dedicated environmentalists—and most, in their recreation of choice, are hikers. However, over the long years of a career they consciously or unconsciously bend toward the source of operating funds. Receipts from timber sales, the large road budget and tiny trail budget voted by Congress, and the steady pressure from Washington City (responding to industry influence in the White House) to increase the logging of roadless areas, thus destroying trails, shape the group personality of the bureaucracy.

In the state of Washington, the lean toward machines is magnified by the insidious bill that hired hands of the motorcycle lobby got through the state legislature, giving a brandnew bureaucracy composed of ATV–ORV fans a year-after-year cornucopia of tax revenues—including taxes paid by hikers—to convert hiker trails to motorcycle roads.

The conundrum of the Forest Service is that though they know hikers are far and away the major users of trails, they also see that hikers make no direct, highly visible contribution of money, as do their competitors; they share the faceless anonymity of the American Taxpayer. As a result, trails dedicated to their sole use steadily deteriorate. An example is the Annette Lake trail (Hike 2). Used by 6000 hikers a year, the trail was rebuilt in 1986 at a cost of $5,000 per mile; sadly, no maintenance funds were to be had, the trail eroded, and the capital investment was lost.

How, then, are hikers to "get along"? Not by meekly thanking their employees in government for small mercies. As the old mule-skinner answered when asked why he never gave his team a command without first conking their heads with a club, "First you have to get their attention." For nigh on to a half-century, hikers have been systematically abused and maltreated and excluded in favor of logging trucks and jeeps and ATVs and dirtbikes and, now, "mountain bikes," all in the name of "multiple-use." That's not getting along, that's being stomped on.

Nevertheless, hikers are more than eager to share the Message of the Wildlands with those who wish to hear. But listeners old and new cannot be dumped one atop the other. Land-managers, federal, state, and local, cannot be allowed to get away with a quick fix—they cannot reclassify hiker trails as "multi-use trails"; in a crowded world there is no such critter except in the minds of bureaucrats. At a time when the numbers of walkers, hikers, and backpackers are rising steadily, the trail miles available to them cannot be decreased. Horse-riders, too, must not have their historical rights diminished. As for the new travel modes, if land-managers deem the terrains under their jurisdiction tough enough to withstand motorcycles and ATVs, or "mountain bikes" and all-terrain rollerskates, they must devise new and separate routes.

All parties to the debate should bite the bullet: *It may prove that the wild world is not big enough for everybody to do his own thing just because it feels good*. Hikers have accepted that they cannot, on the whim of the moment, camp at Lake Constance, cannot camp at all in Snowgrass Flat, cannot even enter portions of the ruins of Mount St. Helens. Recognizing that their numbers are too large for them to enjoy the free-and-easy life of the past, they are that much less content to be driven off trails by newcomers who are as ignorant of the historical continuity of the wilderness as a 2-year-old child is of the world of his parents, and just as selfishly determined to scream and howl until they get what they want, reasonable or not, fair or not.

There probably is room on earth for motorcycles and "mountain bikes," but certainly not on historic hiker–horse trails. The newcomers must cease striving to conquer the routes of the older uses and labor to establish new routes for their new modes of travel.

Money

Beginning hikers, experienced hikers, horse people, bicyclists, ORVers, cross-country skiers, snowmobilers, and the handicapped all have their special need that takes money. Of special interest to hikers is finding funds to separate conflicting uses such as bicycles and ORVs and building trails outside wilderness to relieve the overuse within.

It is doubtful that Congress will ever fully fund forest recreation, so where is the funding to come from? A recent poll showed many hikers leaning toward user fees, providing they go to recreation and not the general fund.

How You Can Help

Environmental organizations have considerable clout in the lobbies of Congress, and thank golly for that. However, so desperate is the status of ancient forests, wild rivers, and wildlife that these advocates have little energy to spend on lobbying for trail protection and trail funding. As for organizations focused on foot trails, they have next to no clout because most people take to the trail by twos and threes and feel no need to join a club. The State of Washington has an estimated 1,000,000 hikers and backpackers; fewer than 1 percent belong to any trail-advocacy group.

Your individual letters to the Forest Service and to your congressmen are all the more important. Unless you belong to a trail-protection organization, you are unlikely to have much advance notice of threats. When you do hear about a trail-destruction plan, write a thoughtful, constructive, polite letter to the appropriate agency. Don't be dismayed when you are answered with a form letter. Chances are, sometime in the future, a friend in the district ranger's office will use your letter to convince his supervisor that a change is needed.

The historic Enchanted Valley Chalet (Hike 95)

TRAIL OBITUARIES

(A representative sample, not the full slaughter)

Miles	Trail
8.0	Naches Wagon Road—killed by logging roads and jeeps
4.0	Blue Lake trail No. 271—killed by motorcycles and four-wheelers
8.7	Bishop Ridge trail No. 272—killed by motorcycles
3.0	Hamilton Butte trail No. 118—killed by motorcycles and four-wheelers
10.2	Langille Ridge trail No. 259—killed by motorcycles
3.0	Dark Meadows trail No. 263—killed by motorcycles
9.0	Summit Prairie trail No. 1—killed by motorcycles
20.1	Boundary trail No. 1, east end—killed by motorcycles
8.0	Quartz Creek Ridge trail No. 1A—killed by motorcycles
2.6	Staler Camp trail No. 3—killed by motorcycles
9.1	Wright Meadows trail No. 80—killed by logging roads and motorcycles
5.0	Table Mountain trail No. 8—killed by motorcycles
2.5	Green Mountain trail No. 110—killed by motorcycles
5.9	Squaw Creek trail No. 265—killed by motorcycles
2.9	Wobbly Creek trail No. 273—killed by motorcycles
4.4	Krous Ridge trail No. 275—killed by motorcycles
1.7	Rough trail No. 283—killed by motorcycles
4.0	Cussed Hollow trail No. 19—killed by logging roads and motorcycles
3.8	Dry Creek trail No. 289—killed by motorcycles
5.5	Tongue Mountain trail No. 294—killed by motorcycles
2.7	Snipes Mountain trail No. 11—killed by motorcycles
4.8	Squaw trail No. 21—killed by motorcycles
6.0	Middle trail No. 26—killed by motorcycles
3.0	Gotchen trail No. 40—killed by motorcycles
2.4	Buck Creek trail No. 54—killed by motorcycles
2.7	Pine Way trail No. 71—killed by motorcycles
6.0	Morrison Creek trail No. 52—killed by motorcycles
6.8	Monte Carlo trail No. 52—killed by motorcycles
6.8	Monte Cristo trail No. 53—killed by motorcycles
2.5	Spring Creek trail No. 115—killed by motorcycles
3.2	High Lakes trail No. 116—killed by motorcycles
2.5	Paradise trail No. 124—killed by motorcycles
3.0	McClellen Meadows trail No. 159—killed by motorcycles
3.0	Summit Spring trail No. 173—killed by motorcycles

A Note About Safety

Safety is an important concern in all outdoor activities. No guidebook can alert you to every hazard or anticipate the limitations of every reader. Therefore, the descriptions of roads, trails, routes, and natural features in this book are not representations that a particular place or excursion will be safe for your party. When you follow any of the routes described in this book, you assume responsibility for your own safety. Under normal conditions, such excursions require the usual attention to traffic, road and trail conditions, weather, terrain, the capabilities of your party, and other factors. Keeping informed on current conditions and exercising common sense are the keys to a safe, enjoyable outing.

The Mountaineers

Near Hole in the Wall (Hike 99)

McCLELLAN BUTTE

Round trip 9 miles
Hiking time 7 hours
High point 5162 feet
Elevation gain 3700 feet

Hikable July through October
One day
Map: Green Trails Bandera (No. 206)

The sharp little peak looks formidable from Interstate 90, and because of avalanche snows in a gully it can be dangerous until early July. However, a steep and rugged trail climbs to a viewpoint a few feet below the rocky summit for panoramas west over lowlands to Seattle, Puget Sound, and the Olympics, south over uncountable clearcuts to Mt. Rainier, and east to Snoqualmie Pass peaks. The lower part of the route contains numerous scars and artifacts of man's present and past activities; the recorded history of the area dates from 1853, when Captain George B. McClellan journeyed approximately this far up the valley during his search for a cross-Cascades pass for Indian-fighters and immigrants. The trail is very popular even though it gets little maintenance, is badly eroded, and, at best, is difficult.

Drive Interstate 90 to Exit 42, signed "West Tinkham Road," and go off on road No. 55. Immediately beyond the Snoqualmie River bridge, pass the highway workshop and turn right to the trailhead and parking lot, elevation 1500 feet.

Trail No. 1015 follows remnants of a wire-wrapped wooden waterline to a bridge over Alice Creek, climbs a bit, crosses a powerline swath, enters woods again, reaches a long-abandoned, overgrown railroad grade,

Bleeding heart

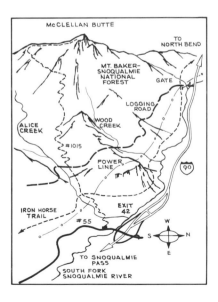

Interstate 90 from summit ridge of McClellan Butte

and at ½ mile crosses the abandoned Milwaukee Railroad grade, now the Iron Horse Trail, and enters an old clearcut. In the woods again, at 1 mile, 2200 feet, cross a private logging road.

The grade steepens, going by a sometime spring in a cool grove of big old trees, and then switchbacks up the wooded north face of the butte. At about 2½ miles the trail rounds the east side of the butte and crosses an avalanche gully whose treacherous snowbank usually lasts into July. From here, with numerous switchbacks, the way sidehills below cliffs and occasional views, attaining the south ridge of the peak at 4 miles, 4500 feet. The route follows the crest a short bit at the edge of large clear-cuts in Seattle's Cedar River Watershed, rounds the east side of the mountain, drops 100 feet to a small pond (possible campsites), and climbs again to a magnificent viewpoint on the ridge crest about 100 vertical feet from the summit.

The majority of hikers are content with the ridge-top view and leave the summit for experienced mountaineers; the rocks are slippery when wet, and in any conditions the exposure is sufficient to be fatal.

Annette Lake and cliffs of Abiel Peak

2 ANNETTE LAKE

Round trip 7½ miles
Hiking time 4 hours
High point 3500 feet
Elevation gain 1500 feet

Hikable June through November
One day or backpack
Map: Green Trails Snoqualmie
Pass (No. 207)

A very popular and often crowded little subalpine lake, with cliffs and talus of Abiel Peak above the shores of open forest. For lonesome walking try early summer or late fall in the middle of the week in terrible weather.

Drive Interstate 90 toward Snoqualmie Pass to Exit 47, signed "Denny Creek." Go off the freeway and turn right 0.1 mile, and then left on road No. 55 for 0.4 mile to the parking lot, elevation 2000 feet.

The way starts in an old clearcut, crosses Humpback Creek, and in 1 mile passes under a powerline and enters forest. At 1¼ miles, 2400 feet, cross the abandoned Milwaukee Railroad grade, now the Iron Horse Trail.

Now comes the hard part, switchbacking steeply upward in old forest on the slopes of Silver Peak. At one point an uprooted tree becomes a broad walkway and occasional talus openings give looks over the valley to Humpback Mountain. After gaining 1200 feet in 2½ miles, at the 3600-foot level a small creek is crossed and the grade flattens out for the final mile of minor ups and downs to the lake outlet, 3¾ miles, 3500 feet.

Wander along the east shore for picnic spots with views of small cliffs and a waterfall that drops into the lake.

Some cross-country hikers continue to the summits of Silver and Abiel Peaks, the route simple enough but quite brushy.

Folks planning to camp do well to call the Forest Service beforehand to learn where and how they can; the lake is so mobbed that great care is being taken to avoid making it a muddy/dusty slum.

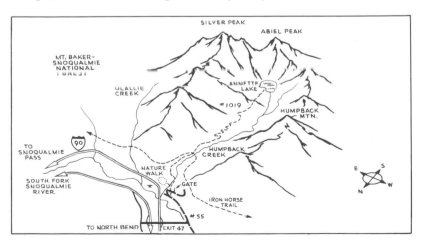

3
COLD CREEK–
SILVER PEAK LOOP

Loop trip 6 miles
Hiking time 3½ hours
High point 4400 feet
Elevation gain 1400 feet
One day
Map: Green Trails Snoqualmie
    Pass (No. 207)

Sidetrip up Silver Peak 2 miles
Hiking time 2 hours
High point 5603 feet
Elevation gain 1400 feet
Hikable July through October

Grand trees, a mountain lake, and a summit with great views south over rolling green ridges to Rainier, west to the Olympics (Annette Lake directly below your feet), north to Snoqualmie Pass peaks, and east across Keechelus Reservoir to Mt. Margaret, so patched by clearcuts it looks as if it had a bad case of the mange.

Though much of the old beauty remains, long gone are the challenge and the remoteness that until a quarter-century ago made this one of the most popular hikes near Snoqualmie Pass. This is in the checkerboard dating from the Big Steal, the Northern Pacific Land Grant, and logging roads are built by private owners. Despite management problems the Forest Service has made a sincere effort at true multiple-use—which means trails, too.

Drive Interstate 90 east from Snoqualmie Pass 2 miles and go off on Hyak Exit 54. Turn right and then left into the large Pacific West–Hyak ski area parking lot. Halfway through the lot, go left on a road obscurely signed "Hyak Estates Division 3 and 4." Pass houses and go to the right of the Wastewater Treatment Plant where the way becomes Forest Service road No. 9070. At 1 mile keep left at a junction on road No. 9070. At 3.3 miles from I-90 is Cold Creek trailhead, signed "Twin Lakes," elevation 3000 feet.

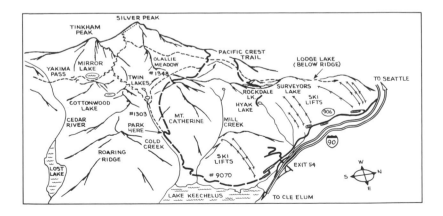

Mount Rainier from Silver Peak, Abiel Peak on right

(If your sole interest is the ascent of Silver, stay on No. 9070 another 2 miles to where it crosses the Pacific Crest Trail at Olallie Meadow, 4200 feet. Walk the Crest Trail south 1½ miles to the Gardiner Ridge Trail, as noted below.)

Alternating between clearcuts and forest, Silver Peak standing 2300 feet above it all, Cold Creek trail No. 1303 attains lower Twin Lake at about ¾ mile. Here is a junction. Go either direction—the loop has as much uphill one way as the other. We describe it clockwise because that's how we happened to do it.

Cross the outlet stream and grind out 1300 feet in 1¾ miles to the Pacific Crest Trail and the 4400-foot high point 2½ miles from the road (sign says "2"). Turn right (north). For the sidetrip ascent of Silver Peak, in an up-and-down ½ mile watch carefully for the sign marking Gardiner Ridge Trail, an old route to Hanson Creek that was abandoned because it is partly in the Cedar River Watershed. Easy to miss, the sidetrail gains 600 feet in a scant ½ mile (that seems a long 1 mile) to heather-and-shrub parkland. The mountainside is broken by a large talus; some hikers go straight up the rocks but skirting them left or right is easier. Above the talus follow the flowery ridge crest, then 200 feet of steep, shattered rock to the 5603-foot summit.

Returned from the sidetrip ascent to the Pacific Crest Trail, continue northward to road No. 9070 at Olallie Meadow, turn right on it about 400 feet, find trail No. 1348, and follow it 1 mile back to Twin Lakes and so home.

4   SUMMIT LAKE

Round trip to Summit Lake 5
  miles
Hiking time 3 hours
High point 5400 feet
Elevation gain 1200 feet

Hikable July through October
One day or backpack
Map: Green Trails Enumclaw
  (No. 237)

An alpine lake, but don't be misled by the name—it's not on the summit of anything. However, there are flower fields and a fabulous view of Mt. Rainier.

Drive SR 410 to a complicated intersection at the southwest corner of Buckley, turn south on SR 162 for 1½ miles, turn left on SR 165, and proceed another 17 miles, following signs to "Carbon River Entrance, Mount Rainier National Park," passing Wilkeson, Carbonado, and the one-lane bridge over the Carbon River. At 8.4 miles SR 165 goes uphill toward Mowich Lake; stay left on the Carbon River Road. Just before reaching the entrance to Mount Rainier National Park, turn left on road No. 7810, cross the Carbon River on wooden bridges, and climb 5.3 miles to a junction with road No. 7820. Keep left, staying on No. 7810, and at 6.7 miles reach the road-end and the Bearhead Mountain and Summit Lake trail No. 1177, elevation 4300 feet.

Constantly climbing, the trail starts up through a clearcut, makes a big switchback, and enters dense forest, which cuts off sights and sounds of encroaching logging and automobiles. At 1 mile enter the Clearwater Wilderness and soon reach wooded Twin Lake, 4800 feet (there is only one lake), and a junction with Carbon trail No. 1179 (Hike 5); keep left on No. 1177.

The path crosses the outlet and heads uphill, passing subalpine ponds or marshes, depending on the season. Nearly at the top of the ridge, the way traverses the slopes on a fairly level grade, at one point emerging from timber into a small meadow with a view of Rainier. At 2½ miles,

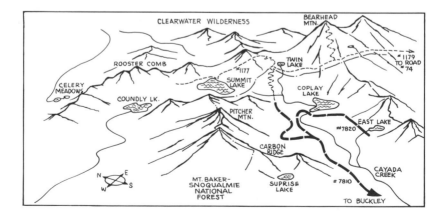

Summit Lake and Mount Rainier (John Spring photo)

5400 feet, Summit Lake is attained. Bordering the shores are open fields of beargrass and, in season, a brilliant garden of flowers. Campsites are scattered in the trees. To preserve the vegetation, hikers must camp 100 feet from the shore.

No open fires are allowed in the Summit Lake Basin. Backpackers who have no stove and need a cooking fire should stay on the righthand shore to find campsites ¼ mile beyond the lake, toward the Rooster Comb, and walk back to the lake to fetch water.

For the first and most essential sidetrip, follow the trail around the lake, find a steep path to the top of a 5737-foot hill, and look down to Coplay Lake. The view of Mt. Rainier is grand above—and equally broad of the mindboggling panorama of logging below.

5 BEARHEAD MOUNTAIN

Round trip 6½ miles
Hiking time 4 hours
High point 6089 feet
Elevation gain 1800 feet

Hikable July through October
One day
Map: Green Trails Enumclaw
(No. 237)

The highest point in the Clearwater Wilderness is an old lookout site rising above meadows that in late July and early August are a riot of color—the brilliant blue of lupine, the red of paintbrush, and the rainbow hues of species that would fill a flower book. Equally stunning are the miles upon miles of clearcuts to the west; north and east are fractions of miles of virgin forest saved from the chainsaw at the last minute. Yet the eye is hard-pressed to focus on all this, what with the competition of the Great North (Willis) Wall of Mt. Rainier. Even from this distance the avalanches are awesome, the more so because few of the monstrous masses of tumbling ice can be heard.

Drive to the Summit Lake–Bearhead trailhead, elevation 4300 feet, as described in Hike 4.

Hike trail No. 1177 through a clearcut and up switchbacks 1 long mile, enter the Clearwater Wilderness, and proceed a bit farther to tiny Twin Lake and a junction, 4800 feet. The left fork is to Summit Lake; go right on Carbon trail No. 1179, which contours and climbs another long mile around steep slopes to the ridge top and a second junction at 5400 feet. Go left ¾ mile on trail No. 1179A to the summit. Settle down and spread out your lunch. Your eyes, too, will feast.

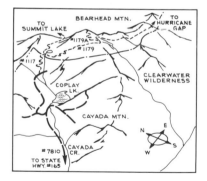

Beargrass

Mount Rainier from lookout site on Bearhead Mountain

**GREENWATER RIVER—
ECHO LAKE**

Round trip 14 miles
Hiking time 7 hours
High point 4100 feet
Elevation gain 1640 feet

Hikable May through mid
   November at lower elevations
One day or backpack
Map: Green Trails Lester (No. 239)

Once one of the most famous cathedrals of old-growth Douglas fir out-side a national park or dedicated wilderness, among the grandest valley forests in the nation, the Greenwater greenery has been whacked down and shipped overseas by loggers—though they knew full well as they were whacking that in several years the valley would be purchased and installed in the gallery of American treasures. The Norse Peak Wilder-ness, which came just too late, has saved a sample, a jewel the more pre-cious for being set amid a butcher shop of "free enterprise." Amid the lingering big trees are sparkling forest lakes and a lovely subalpine lake.

Drive SR 410 east of Enumclaw past Federation Forest State Park to the hamlet of Greenwater. Continue 2 miles and turn left on road No. 70. At 8.4 miles from the highway cross the Greenwater, go another 0.4 mile, and turn right on road No. 7033 to the trailhead, elevation 2600 feet.

Follow Greenwater trail No. 1176 across the clearcut to the edge and enter a magnificence of old trees thrusting high above a rich understory of devil's club, vanilla leaf, trillium, and moss—much, much moss. (Yet just a short way up the steep valley walls on either side is loggers' "day-light," and from it the storm waters formerly held back by forest are car-rying gravel and boulders and logging slash down to the river.)

At ¾ mile the trail crosses the Greenwater and at 1½ miles recrosses at the first of the two little Meeker (Greenwater) Lakes. The second is at 2 miles. At 3½ miles the trail reaches a junction with Lost Creek trail No. 1185, a 3-mile sidetrip to Lost Lake. So far the trail has gained only 200 feet a mile, but near the 5-mile mark it leaves the valley bottom and

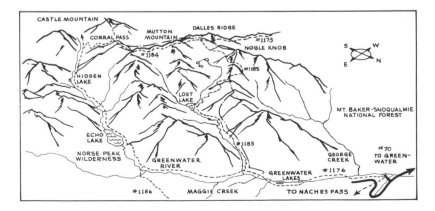

Greenwater River crossing

starts climbing in earnest. At 5½ miles pass a junction with trail No.
1186. At 6½ miles cross a 4100-foot high point and drop 300 feet to the
edge of 3819-foot Echo Lake, surrounded by wooded hills with a glimpse
of meadows and craggy peaks of Castle Mountain.

The trail continues 6 miles to Corral Pass. The entire route, near lakes
and along river, offers numerous campsites. At Echo Lake campers must
keep 100 feet from the water; the west shore is closed.

7 NOBLE KNOB

Round trip 7 miles
Hiking time 5 hours
High point 6011 feet
Elevation gain 500 feet in, 300 feet
  out

Hikable July through October
One day or backpack
Map: Green Trails Lester (No. 239)

If you want flowers, burn the trees. As the result of a fire set by lightning (or somebody) in the 1920s, the fields of color here rival those of Paradise. In stark contrast to the at-hand yellows and blues and reds is the whiteness of the north side of Mt. Rainier, not far away across the valley, close enough to see crevasses in the Emmons Glacier and cinders of the crater rim.

The trail lies along the edge of Norse Peak Wilderness, occasionally dipping into the preserve, meaning at least part of the trail will be free from machines. Note the extensive rehabilitation work done by the Forest Service in meadows ravaged by jeepers and motorcyclists—destroyers that should not have been allowed in the first place.

Drive SR 410 east 30 miles from the White River Ranger Station in Enumclaw to just 1.5 miles short of Mount Rainier National Park and turn up road No. 7174, signed "Corral Pass Campground" (sign missing in 1990). Ascend very steeply 5.8 miles to Noble Knob trail No. 1184, elevation 5700 feet.

The trail contours a hillside, alternating ¾ mile between flowers and groves of subalpine trees, and then follows the now-abandoned jeep road another ¾ mile. A short, abrupt bit concludes with a resumption of trail. At 2 miles pass Deep Creek trail No. 1196, and at 2½ miles reach a 5900-foot saddle. The trail now drops steadily. At 3 miles, directly above Twentyeight Mile Lake, pass Dalles Ridge trail No. 1178. Shortly beyond, at 5600 feet, is a three-way junction.

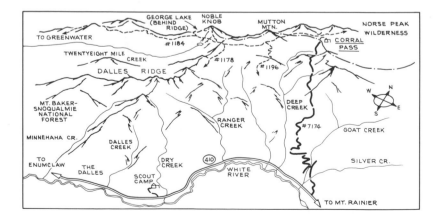

Mount Rainier from Noble Knob trail

The left fork, trail No. 1184, descends past George Lake (a mile from the junction a sidepath contours right to the lake, 5500 feet, and campsites) to road No. 72. The right fork goes down past Lost Lake to the Greenwater Trail (Hike 6). Take the middle trail, cross a large meadow, and, with one switchback in a path overgrown in blossoms, traverse completely around the mountain to the old lookout site atop 6011-foot Noble Knob.

8 BIG CROW BASIN–NORSE PEAK

Round trip to Norse Peak 10 miles
Hiking time 6 hours
High point 6856 feet
Elevation gain 3000 feet

Hikable late June through early
   November
One day
Maps: Green Trails Bumping
   Lake (No. 271), Lester (No. 239)

Lovely alpine meadows, one with a small lake, offer a wonderful weekend of wandering. However, the shortest way to the basin involves climbing nearly to the top of 6856-foot Norse Peak—an arduous backpack. Most hikers therefore settle for a day trip to the summit, an abandoned lookout site, and enjoy the views down to the inviting gardens and all around to panoramas extending from Snoqualmie Pass peaks to Mt. Adams, from golden hills of Eastern Washington to green lowlands of Puget Sound. The trail to Norse Peak usually is open for walking in late June; the meadow country remains under snow until mid-July. Horse use on

Crystal Mountain ski area from Norse Peak

trails has increased drastically due to a concessionaire and the tread has deteriorated to boulders and deep ruts.

Drive SR 410 east some 33 miles from Enumclaw to Silver Springs summer homes. A bit beyond, just before the Mount Rainier National Park boundary, turn left toward the Crystal Mountain ski area. At 4 miles, 3900 feet, park beside the highway. If no room, drive 0.3 mile farther and go right to the horse camp trailhead and parking area.

Find the old mine-to-market road, No. (7190)410, walk it about 1000 feet, and go off left on trail No. 1191. Very soon the tip of Mt. Rainier appears over the ridge to the west and every additional step reveals more of the mountain. By 2 miles the whole summit is in sight and the scene steadily expands as more elevation is gained. The route is confused here and there by crisscrossing of the old tread—take the path of least resistance, which generally is the new trail. At 4 miles, 6600 feet, the summit ridge is topped and a junction reached.

The right fork follows the ridge crest 1 mile to Norse Peak. Look northeast into Big Crow Basin and east to Lake Basin and appealing Basin Lake. Look down to the Crystal Mountain ski area, one of the favorites in the coastal Northwest; unfortunately, snow doesn't last all year and the summer view is a hodgepodge of bulldozer tracks.

The left fork drops eastward 1 mile to join the Pacific Crest Trail, which descends ½ mile to Big Crow Basin; at about 5700 feet are a shelter cabin and good camping, though water may be scarce in late summer. Partway down find a sidetrail leading over a low green ridge to Basin Lake, 6200 feet.

The meadow and peak also can be approached by way of the Bullion Basin Trail, intersecting the Pacific Crest Trail at Blue Bell Pass.

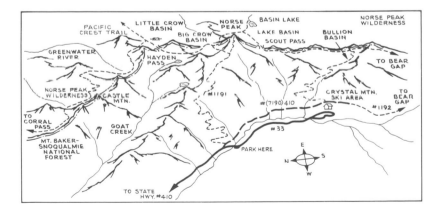

9 CRYSTAL MOUNTAIN LOOP

Round trip to viewpoint 6 miles
Hiking time 3½ hours
High point 5500 feet
Elevation gain 1300 feet
Hikable July through September
One day
Map: Green Trails Bumping Lake
(No. 271)

Loop trip 8 miles
Hiking time 5 hours
High point 6552 feet
Elevation gain 2450 feet

Along the boundary of Mount Rainier National Park, a Forest Service trail wanders through striking views of Rainier and the White River. Flowers in one season, huckleberries in another. Hikers who get up early enough in the morning have a good chance of seeing elk; those starting late must dodge bicycles and horses.

The trip comes in two versions: one afoot both uphill and downhill, the other using the Crystal Mountain chairlift for the uphill, a trail–road combination for the downhill. Both will be described here, the "normal" version first.

From SR 410 at the park boundary near Silver Springs summer homes, turn left on the Crystal Mountain Highway. Drive 4.3 miles and turn right on road No. (7190)410 for 0.4 mile to the trailhead and horse-unloading ramp, elevation 4100 feet.

Trail No. 1163 begins as a service road under a powerline but soon becomes legitimate, climbing gently through clearcuts, then an old burn, in loose, dusty, pumice soil. Shade is scarce and water nonexistent. (Did you remember to fill the canteen?) Heat and thirst are forgotten when, in 3 miles, at 5500 feet, the crest of Crystal Mountain is attained and Mt. Rainier overpowers the horizon. This is a great place to soak up the view and go home.

However, if impelled by the bearish urge to see the other side of the next rise, carry on. The ridge varies from narrow, a cliff on the park side, to broad and rounded. Below the meadow crest are vast fields of huckleberries. And the views! Chances are a party will find ample rewards long

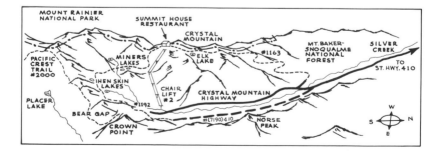

White River and Mount Rainier from Crystal Ridge

before completing the 3 steady-climbing ridge-crest miles to the top terminal of Chair No. 2, 6 miles from the road.

For the loop trip's mixture of lakes, meadows, and huckleberries, descend a service road that starts near the terminal. In ⅓ mile find legitimate trail No. 1163, switchbacking down through Silver Queen Basin, past Hen Skin Lakes, to a junction with Silver Creek trail No. 1192. Follow it 1 mile to an old mining road, No. (7190)410, descend this 2 miles to Crystal Mountain Highway, cross the pavement, and return to the starting point.

Now for the all-downhill tour. (Let it be noted this version is no good for elk-watching—by the time of day the chairlifts start running, the animals have finished eating and retired to the forest to chew their cuds.) Drive to the ski area parking lot, elevation 4200 feet, ride Chair No. 2 to the top, elevation 6776 feet, find the Crystal Ridge Trail, and hike either way. Both are so interesting and different that you may want to go back a second time for the other direction or, as we did, start early in the morning so you can see the elk and hike the whole loop at one go.

10 SOURDOUGH GAP

Round trip 6 miles
Hiking time 4 hours
High point 6400 feet
Elevation gain 1100 feet in, 200
feet out

Hikable July through October
One day or backpack
Maps: Green Trails Mt. Rainier
(No. 270), Bumping Lake
(No. 271)

A delightful bit of the Pacific Crest Trail (probably the easiest meadow walk in this entire book) through flower gardens and grassy fields to a high pass. A good overnight hike for beginners, except that camping space is limited and very crowded on weekends. Do the trip in early August when flowers are at their peak.

Drive SR 410 east from Enumclaw or west of Yakima to the summit of Chinook Pass, 5432 feet. Just outside Mount Rainier National Park's boundary, find the Pacific Crest trailhead parking lot around the bend in the highway. (Vandalism of cars left overnight is a problem.)

Follow the Pacific Crest Trail northward paralleling the highway, dropping slightly in the first mile, at times on cliffs almost directly above the road. At about 1½ miles the way rounds a ridge, leaves the highway, and starts a gentle climb to Sheep Lake, 2½ miles, 5700 feet—a great place to camp if not crowded. But it almost always is, and the meadows have been badly damaged. Find better camping on benches a few hundred feet away.

The moderate ascent continues through flowers, a final long switchback leading to Sourdough Gap, 3 miles, 6400 feet. (At about 500 feet below the gap, the summit of Mt. Rainier can be seen briefly between two peaks to the west.)

Views from the gap are limited. For broader vistas, continue on the trail another ⅓ mile, descending a little to a small pass with looks down Morse Creek to Placer Lake, an artificial reservoir dammed up by miners years ago.

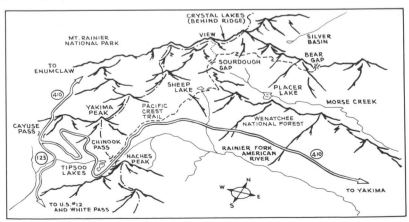

Sheep Lake

Crossing North Fork Union Creek

⊤⊤ UNION CREEK

Round trip 8 miles
Hiking time 4 hours
High point 4500 feet
Elevation gain 1300 feet in, 400
feet out

Hikable late June through
October
One day or backpack
Map: Green Trails Bumping Lake
(No. 271)

A pleasant valley walk through forests by a mountain stream is highlighted by superb falls. The woodland camps beside the waters where the ouzels dip-dip-dip are more comfortable from July on, when the snow has melted and the meltwater dried up.

From Chinook Pass drive SR 410 east, passing Lodgepole Campground at 7.4 miles; at 9.2 miles between mileposts 78 and 79, just before the highway crosses Union Creek, turn left on an unsigned forest road a few hundred feet to the start of trail No. 956, elevation 3500 feet. (From Yakima drive SR 410 west about 10 miles from Bumping River junction to Union Creek.)

In ¼ mile look up Union Creek to a large waterfall. After the trail crosses the creek and commences switchbacks, two spurs drop to the falls, both worth investigating, the second the more exciting. The trail climbs 600 feet in the first mile, often steeply, and then goes up and down to another fine falls on North Fork Union Creek, crossed on a bridge at the falls' top. Downhill some and uphill more, the way ascends to 4500 feet, and then loses altitude to the creek level at 4 miles and campsites, 4250 feet.

The trail follows the creek closely almost ½ mile before beginning a long, steep uphill to Cement Basin trail No. 987 at 6½ miles and the Pacific Crest Trail at 7 miles, near Bluebell Pass and remains of the old Bluebell Mine.

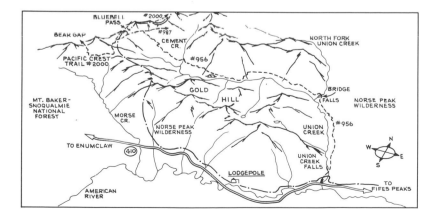

12   CROW LAKE WAY

Round trip to Grassy Saddle 10 miles
Hiking time 8 hours
High point 5900 feet
Elevation gain 2700 feet in, 500 feet out

Hikable early June to hunting season
One day or backpack
Map: Green Trails Bumping Lake (No. 271)

A steep trail, with no water except that carried in canteens, climbs from valley forests to high meadows, compensating for the sweat and struggle by offering exciting views of the needlelike spires of Fifes Peaks and the meanders of the American River. The route can be continued past pretty little Grassy Saddle to the large, boggy meadows surrounding Crow Creek Lake, a favorite haunt of throngs of elk and deer. The animals are fun to watch in the summer but are best steered clear of in the season when hunters outnumber the huntees.

Drive SR 410 east of Chinook Pass some 12.5 miles (1.5 miles east of Pleasant Valley Campground) and between mileposts 81 and 82 find the trailhead on the left side of the road, elevation 3400 feet.

Crow Lake Way No. 953 enters Norse Peak Wilderness several hundred feet from the highway, and commences a long, steady uphill haul, gaining 2200 feet in 3½ miles. The trail begins with switchbacks climbing through forest to a hogback, which then is followed (with glimpses of Fifes Peaks) by dramatic drop-offs overlooking American Ridge. The views grow step by step to a 5800-foot high point at 4 miles, a good turnaround for day trippers.

The trail swings into Survey Creek drainage and at 4½ miles crosses a broad divide, 5900 feet, to Crow Creek drainage. West are rolling green meadows inviting a tour. At about 5 miles, 5600 feet, are Grassy Saddle, a small creek, and, half-hidden in trees, a very small lake. Campsites nearby are great bases for explorations.

For the first, roam the basin at the head of Falls Creek. The unmarked

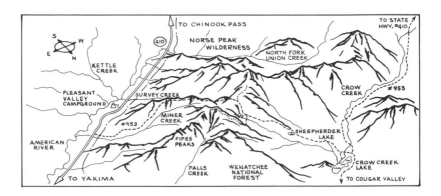

Fifes Peaks from Crow Lake Way

trail starts at the far end of the lake, skirts a rockslide, and climbs to the
basin edge at 6400 feet. The basin rim can be followed like the lip of a cup
in a semicircle to cliffs of Fifes Peaks. Other explorations are the 6400-
foot hill to the west and, longer, the 3 miles along Crow Lake Way, in
green meadows, to Crow Creek Lake.

13

FIFES RIDGE

Round trip to first viewpoint 6 miles
Hiking time 8 hours
High point 5400 feet
Elevation gain 1100 feet

Hikable May through October
One day or backpack
Map: Green Trails Bumping Lake (No. 271)

Overlook the spectacular cliffs and pinnacles of Fifes Peaks. Gaze around the horizon to Rainier, Stuart, Adams, and Goat Rocks. Direct your eyes past the tips of your toes, down to silvery wanderings of the American River, where you came from. Lift your eyes to American Ridge, across the valley in the companion William O. Douglas Wilderness.

From Chinook Pass drive SR 410 east 13.5 miles, 2.6 miles beyond Pleasant Valley Campground; between mileposts 82 and 83, find the trailhead parking area on the uphill side of the highway near Wash Creek, elevation 3320 feet. (From Yakima drive SR 410 west 2.5 miles beyond the Bumping Lake junction.)

Fifes Ridge trail No. 954 climbs moderately along the west bank of Wash Creek about 1 mile, takes a deep breath, and tilts the angle to gain 1800 feet in the next 2 miles—fortunately, in forest shade. At 1½ miles Wash Creek is crossed and at 2 miles recrossed.

At 2¾ miles the trail tops Fifes Ridge at an unmarked junction. If your trip is an overnight backpack, go straight ahead, descending 300 feet and contouring to camps along Falls Creek. For the high views turn right and continue up, at 3 miles gaining a 5400-foot bare knoll and first viewpoint of the dramatic south face of Fifes Peaks. Fill your eyes but continue 2 miles, up and down Fifes Ridge, to a 6315-foot knoll and the climax panoramas.

Old maps show a trail completely around Fifes Peaks. Don't believe it. Whatever path may have existed earlier in the century has long since vanished.

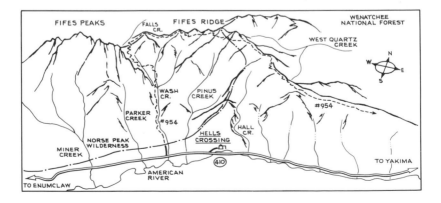

Fifes Peaks from Fifes Ridge trail

14 MESATCHEE CREEK– COUGAR LAKES

Round trip to American Ridge
   11 miles
Hiking time 7 hours
High point 6000 feet
Elevation gain 1000 feet
Hikable mid-July through
   September
One day
Maps: USFS William O. Douglas
   Wilderness, Green Trails
   Bumping Lake (No. 271)

Round trip to Cougar Lakes
   22 miles
Allow 2–3 days
High point 6000 feet
Elevation gain 2900 feet in, 1400
   feet out
Hikable mid-July through
   September
Backpack

The hiking distance to Cougar Lakes is longer by this approach than from the Bumping River (Hike 20). However, the ascent up the creek valley is a proper joy, and the ramble along American Ridge (Hike 15) is the most fun of the whole trip.

Drive SR 410 east from Chinook Pass 6.6 miles, and at milepost 76 turn right 0.4 mile on road No. (1700)460 to Mesatchee Creek trail No. 969, elevation 3600 feet.

The first 1¼ level miles lie along an old road, perhaps partly the original miners' road to Morse Creek. Cross American River on a log, enter William O. Douglas Wilderness, and in 1½ miles intersect Dewey Lake trail No. 968. Go left, staying on No. 969, which gets down to business, switchbacking upward. Mesatchee Creek now can be heard, the sound soon followed by sight of a waterfall and then, at last, the creek. At 2½ miles the way moderates and at 3¾ miles, 4900 feet, crosses the creek to an excellent camp.

The trail traverses a 1929 burn, now a miniaturized Christmas-tree forest of little subalpine fir and western larch. At 4½ miles cross a small stream (limited camping) and at 5½ miles join American Ridge trail No.

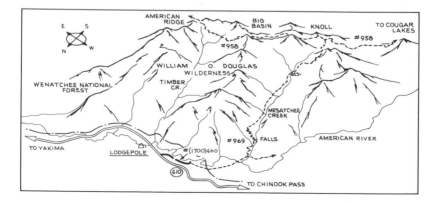

Waterfall on Mesatchee Creek

958, 5850 feet.

It is not compulsory to head for Cougar Lakes—the ridge itself is an excellent destination. Go east a few hundred yards to a knoll with views of Bumping Lake, Mt. Adams, the rugged summits of House Rock, Crag Mountain, Mt. Aix, Bismark Peak, the more rounded Nelson Ridge, and the volcanic cone of Tumac Mountain.

For Cougar Lakes turn west, losing 300 feet, switchbacking up 500 feet over a green meadow to a 6000-foot high point, and descending again, at 9½ miles intersecting Swamp Creek trail No. 970, 5000 feet. Keep straight ahead, shortly passing the American Lake Trail and coming to Cougar Lakes, 11 miles, 5015 feet.

15 AMERICAN RIDGE

Round trip from Goose Prairie to
   viewpoint 12 miles
Hiking time 7 hours
High point 6310 feet
Elevation gain 2950 feet
Hikable June through November
One day or backpack
Maps: USFS William O. Douglas
   Wilderness, Green Trails
   Bumping Lake (No. 271), Old
   Scab Mountain (No. 272)

One-way trip from Goose Prairie
   to Pacific Crest Trail 19 miles
Allow 3 days
High point 6946 feet
Elevation gain 5500 feet
Hikable late July through
   October

As the crow flies, American Ridge is 19 miles long, but with twists, turns, and switchbacks, the trail takes 27 miles to complete the traverse. The way is mostly rough and sometimes steep, but the meadowlands are beautiful and lonesome. Flowers are in full bloom at the east end of the ridge about Memorial Day (the usual time that Chinook Pass opens) and at the west end in early August. The east end makes an excellent early-season trip when other high trails are still snowed in. Look for avalanche and glacier lilies and a rare pink-and-purple flower called steer's head, because that's exactly what it looks like.

The entire ridge is worth hiking, but in June only the east end is free of snow, and by August this stretch is dry and hot. Therefore the recommendation is to hike from Goose Prairie to an intersection with the American Ridge Trail and turn east (in June) or west (in August) along the crest.

Drive SR 410 east from Chinook Pass 19 miles (or west from Yakima) and turn right on the Bumping River road. In 0.6 mile is the eastern trailhead, signed "American Ridge trail No. 958"; if a complete traverse of American Ridge is planned, start here, elevation 2800 feet.

At 9.3 miles from SR 410 find Goose Prairie trail No. 972 on the right side of the road, elevation 3360 feet. Park in a small camp on the left.

The Goose Prairie Trail is in woods all the way, climbing steadily but

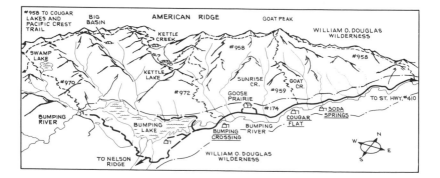

American Ridge and Bumping Lake

never steeply, beginning in fir and pine forest typical of the Cascades' east slopes and ascending into Alaska cedars, subalpine firs, and wind-bent pines. At 1½ miles the path crosses several small streams and ascends a series of nine switchbacks, at 2 miles recrossing the same streams. At 4¾ miles a spring runs most of the summer—possible camping here. At 5 miles the ridge top is attained and so is the intersection with American Ridge trail No. 958, elevation 6200 feet.

Day-hikers (any season) should follow the ridge west, climbing ½ mile to a point where the trail starts down into Kettle Creek drainage. Leave the trail and continue ¼ mile more up the ridge to a 6310-foot knoll with fine views of Mt. Rainier, Mt. Aix, and miles of ridges north and south.

Early-season overnight hikers should turn east, following the ridge through forest and meadows to Goat Peak at 11 miles, site of the former American Ridge Lookout, elevation 6473 feet, and a view of the spectacular cliffs of Fifes Peaks. If transportation has been arranged, a party can continue 7½ miles down to the Bumping River road and the previously mentioned American Ridge trailhead, completing a one-way trip of 18½ miles, an elevation gain of about 3600 feet.

Midsummer and fall overnight hikers should turn west, climbing near the top of the 6310-foot knoll and then descending to campsites at shallow Kettle Lake, 6 miles, 5650 feet. (Below the lake is a small spring.) The trail contours around the head of Kettle Creek, climbing to the ridge crest at 10 miles, 6946 feet, and dropping again to Big Basin at 11 miles, 6300 feet, a cirque with good campsites, bands of elk, and glorious scenery.

With some ups and more downs, the trail follows the ridge top from meadows back into subalpine forest at a low point of 5500 feet, then up to meadowland at 6000 feet and a campsite near Mud Lake at 13½ miles. At 16½ miles is a junction with Swamp Lake trail No. 970, a popular route leading to Cougar Lakes in 1 mile and a steep way trail that joins the Pacific Crest Trail; No. 958 goes right, reaching American Lake at 18 miles and the Crest Trail at 19½ miles.

If transportation can be arranged, a one-way trip can be made via the Crest Trail to Chinook Pass, a total distance of 26½ miles, or via the Swamp Lake Trail to Upper Bumping Road, a total of 21 miles.

Mount Rainier from Goat Peak on American Ridge

16 GOAT PEAK

Round trip 10 miles
Hiking time 6 hours
High point 6473 feet
Elevation gain 3400 feet
Hikable late June through
  October

One day
Maps: USFS William O. Douglas
  Wilderness, Green Trails
  Bumping Lake (No. 271), Old
  Scab Mountain (No. 272)

A former lookout site on the highest summit of 17-mile-long American Ridge gives views down to the American River, north across the valley to impressive cliffs of Fifes Peaks, south over Bumping Reservoir to Aix and Adams, and west over Chinook Pass to Rainier. Four trails converge near the top of Goat Peak. Two are reached from SR 410: trail No. 968B from Pleasant Valley Campground and very steep trail No. 968C from Hells Canyon Campground. The peak is a quick sidetrip for hikers on the American Ridge Trail (Hike 15), but that's a journey of a number of days; trail No. 968, the easiest but not necessarily the shortest approach from the road, is described here. The trail is dry, so carry water; for camping go early in summer when snowmelt rills are running.

Drive SR 410 east 19 miles from Chinook Pass (or west from Yakima) and turn right on Bumping River Road 5.7 miles to Goat Creek trail No. 959, elevation 3100 feet.

The trail, never near the creek for which it is named, briskly climbs steep forest slopes in long and short switchbacks, in 4 strenuous miles intersecting American Ridge trail No. 958. A short distance from the ridge top the views begin.

Go north on the crest 1 mile to a short spur that climbs 300 feet to the summit, 6473 feet. With a second car the return to Bumping River Road can be made by either trail No. 958 or No. 972 (Hike 15).

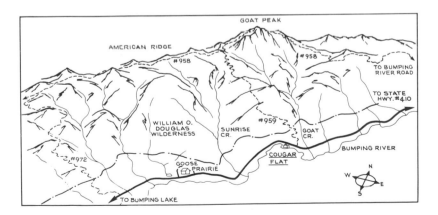

17 COUGAR LAKES

Round trip Cougar Lakes 12 miles
Hiking time 8 hours
High point 5300 feet
Elevation gain 1700 feet in, 300 feet out

Hikable mid-July through October
One day or backpack
Maps: USFS William O. Douglas Wilderness Green Trails Bumping Lake (No. 271)

Two alpine lakes, a big one and a little one, surrounded by generous flower fields in late July and early August, blueberries in early September, and fall colors in October. From ridges above, wide views of Mt. Rainier and the Cascade Crest country. Bumping River must be forded on this approach, not too difficult in the low water of midsummer and early fall, but when spring snows are melted and after the fall monsoons begin, start on either the Bumping Lake Trail on the north side of the lake, adding an extra 4 miles each way, or the Mesatchee Creek Trail (Hike 14), perhaps a better alternative.

Drive SR 410 east from Chinook Pass 19 miles (or west from Yakima), turn right on the Bumping River Road, and follow it 11 miles to the end of pavement at Bumping Lake, at which point the road becomes No. 1800. At 2.5 miles stay on road No. 1800 as it makes a sharp right turn and go another 3.6 miles to the road-end and Swamp Lake trailhead No. 970, elevation 3600 feet.

The flat forest path leads in ½ mile to a ford of the broad and shallow Bumping River, which has very cold water and sharp rocks, so wear wool socks or tennis shoes—or boots without socks, which thus are kept dry for redonning. A bit farther is a junction with the Bumping Lake Trail. Go straight ahead, climbing moderately and steadily in woods and occasional openings to the outlet of Swamp Lake, almost 3¾ miles, 4800 feet;

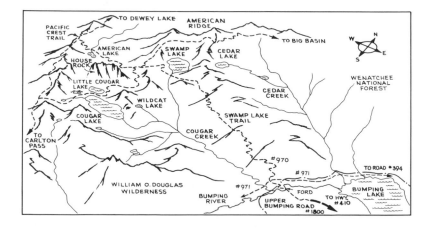

campsites are at and near the shelter cabin.

The trail ascends several hundred feet in ¾ mile to an indistinct divide and a junction with the American Ridge Trail (Hike 15). Go left ¼ mile to another junction. The right-hand trail climbs past American Lake to the Pacific Crest Trail; go left instead, rounding a ridge spur at 5300 feet and dropping into the lake basin, at 6 miles, 5015 feet, reaching the isthmus between the Cougar Lakes.

To the right is Little Cougar Lake, at the foot of the basalt cliffs of House Rock. To the left is Big Cougar Lake. The shores offer numerous legal camps 100 feet from water, but rockfall may menace west-side sites.

For extended horizons, climb a steep and perhaps very muddy mile on the boulder-strewn path leading from the inlet of Big Cougar to the Pacific Crest Trail at 6000 feet. Look for mountain goats, marmots, and rock conies (pikas). For maximum scenery and garden walking, wander north on the Pacific Crest Trail and in about 1½ miles turn right on the trail down to American Lake and back to Cougar Lakes, completing a 5-mile loop.

To preserve the vegetation, camp at least 100 feet from the lakeshores and—whenever possible—200 feet from the Pacific Crest Trail.

Little Cougar Lake and House Rock

BUMPING RIVER

Round trip 16 miles
Allow 2 days
High point 4200 feet
Elevation gain 500 feet, plus many ups and downs

Hikable August through September
One day or backpack
Maps: USFS William O. Douglas Wilderness, Green Trails Bumping Lake (No. 271)

A very easy (except for one bit) forest trail ascends the meandering Bumping River through a valley that is a year-round home of deer and a band of elk, often seen by quiet hikers, and finally rises to the river's source on the Cascade Crest. The walk is magnificent in late June and early July when wildflowers are blooming in the woods; however, that noneasy bit—the ford of the Bumping River—is then downright dangerous, thus the recommendation to wait for the snowmelt to run low.

Drive SR 410 east from Chinook Pass 19 miles (or west from Yakima), turn right on the Bumping River Road, and follow it 11 miles to the end of pavement, at which point the road becomes road No. 1800. In another 2.5 miles stay on road No. 1800 as it makes a sharp right turn and drive another 2.5 miles to Fish Lake Way, trail No. 971A, elevation 3800 feet.

The first 1¾ miles climb a bit and drop some 360 feet to the Bumping River. This much can be hiked in the time of forest flowering without difficulty. However, the horse ford never is absolutely a breeze for pedestrians and until a certain time in summer is a horror. If a person dislikes the look of it, he can bushwhack upstream to see if, by chance, a footlog is available. The final alternative is to drive back to Bumping Lake, drive across the dam to the end of road No. (1800)394, and hike Bumping Lake trail No. 971 4½ miles to the junction of trail No. 971A.

Once across the river the trail is a pussycat. At 2 miles go left on Bumping Lake trail No. 971. At 4½ miles from the road, cross Red Rock Creek on a log to a pair of nice camps, and, at 5½ miles pass a small, nameless lake. The Pacific Crest Trail is attained at 7¾ miles, and, in a final ¼ mile, Fish Lake follows, 4200 feet, shallow and swampy, but with

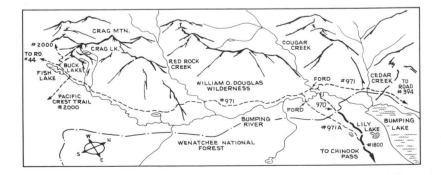

Bumping River

possible campsites.

Before starting home, be sure to sidetrip north on the Crest Trail, climbing 1200 feet to steep and luscious alpine meadows with broad views of volcanoes, active and dormant.

Looking south along Nelson Ridge

BUMPING RIVER
William O. Douglas Wilderness

19   NELSON RIDGE– MOUNT AIX

Round trip to Mt. Aix 12 miles
Hiking time 10 hours
High point 7766 feet
Elevation gain 4200 feet

Hikable mid-June to October
One day
Maps: USFS William O. Douglas
    Wilderness, Green Trails
    Bumping Lake (No. 271)

High gardens in the blue sky of the rainshadow, amid views east to the brown vastness of the heat-hazy Columbia Plateau, west to the shimmering white hugeness of Mt. Rainier, and south along the Cascade Crest to the Goat Rocks and Mt. Adams. Plus closer looks over meadows and forests of the William O. Douglas Wilderness. This is not a beginner's trail—the way is steep, hot, and dry. Carry plenty of liquid.

Drive SR 410 east from Chinook Pass 19 miles (or west from Yakima), turn right on the Bumping Lake Road, and follow it 11 miles to the end of pavement, at which point it becomes road No. 1800. Continue 2.5 miles to a junction. Go straight ahead on road No. 1808 (shown on some maps as No. 395) another 1.5 miles. Just before the Copper Creek bridge, turn left up a steep road signed "Mt. Aix Trail." In a few yards park, elevation 3600 feet.

The merciless trail attains highlands with minimum delay. For openers, the path ascends deep forest nearly to a branch of Copper Creek but never gets to the water, instead switchbacking up a steep hillside. (Across the Copper Creek valley, above Miners Ridge, Rainier appears, and grows with every step.) At 2¼ miles the trail swings into open subalpine forest at the lip of a hanging valley but again never gets to the water. Switchbacks now trend out from the valley into open forest distinguished by superb specimens of whitebark pine.

At 3½ miles is that (last) spring, with a small but cozy campsite gouged from the hillside, more than acceptable when the way beyond is under snow. At nearly 4 miles, 6400 feet, a grassy promontory, with views of Rainier, Adams, and the Goat Rocks, makes a nice campsite in early summer, after snowbanks have melted partly away, while snowmelt is still available. This far makes a satisfying destination for a day hike, especially when slopes above are snowy or the party is pooped.

From the promontory the trail traverses shrubby forest and scree southward and upward to the wide-open crest of Nelson Ridge, 7100 feet, and a choice of wanderings. The up-and-down crest cries out for rambling in either or both directions. The trail contours and climbs a final rocky mile to the summit of 7766-foot Mt. Aix, onetime site of a fire lookout.

Because of their position on the east slope of the Cascades, and the mostly southwest exposures of the trail route, Nelson Ridge and Mt. Aix are free of snow weeks earlier than country a few miles distant. And if the tread at the hanging valley of Copper Creek is all white, as it may be through June, a short and simple detour up amid trees leads back to clear ground. Actually, the maximum flower display comes when patches of snow still linger. The locals consider this trail—whether to the promontory at 4 miles, to Nelson Ridge at 5 miles, or to Mt. Aix at 6 miles—the best early-summer hike in the entire Bumping River area.

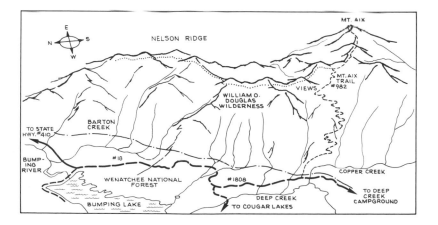

20 TUMAC MOUNTAIN– TWIN SISTERS LAKES

Round trip to Twin Sisters Lakes
 4 miles
Hiking time 2½ hours
High point 5100 feet
Elevation gain 800 feet
Hikable July through October
One day or backpack
**Maps: USFS William O. Douglas Wilderness, Green Trails Bumping
 Lake (No. 271), White Pass (No. 303)**

Round trip to Tumac Mountain
 10½ miles
Hiking time 5 hours
High point 6340 feet
Elevation gain 2050 feet

Hike through alpine meadows by myriad lakes and ponds to the most
varied view of vulcanism in the Washington Cascades. Tumac itself—
postglacial, and probably younger than 10,000 years—is no simple cone
but, rather, built of both cinders and lava and having two craters (both
lake-filled), an infant stratovolcano standing on a broad lava plateau.
This is how mighty Rainier began. The summit presents a panorama of
stratovolcanoes of other ages: Spiral Butte, another infant, at the south
end of the lava plateau; youthful St. Helens, expected by geologists to
grow and violently blow again and again; bulky, mature, deeply dis-
sected Rainier and Adams; and the old, old Goat Rocks, remnant of a
once-mighty Adams-size volcano now reduced to mere roots. Do the climb
in mid-July when upper slopes are covered with red and white heather
plus a peppering of bright red paintbrush. The trip can be 1 day or overnight, camping at one of the lovely Twin Sisters Lakes.

Drive SR 410 east from Chinook Pass 19 miles (or 30 miles from
Naches), turn right on the Bumping River Road, and follow it 11 miles to
the end of pavement, at which point it becomes road No. 1800. Continue
2.5 miles to a junction. Go straight ahead on road No. 1808 (shown on
some maps as No. 395) another 7 miles, passing the horse camp at 6.5

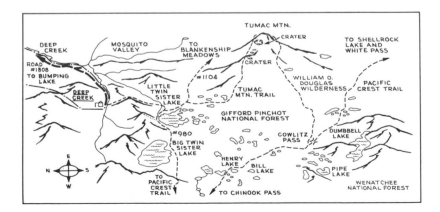

miles, to the road-end at Deep Creek Campground, elevation 4300 feet.

Find Twin Sisters trail No. 980 on the north side of the campground. The way gains 800 feet in 2 miles (all in woods) to the smaller of the Twin Sisters Lakes, 5100 feet.

The "little" lake (only a comparison, both are quite large) has numerous bays and rocky points. To reach the "larger" Twin Sister Lake, follow trail No. 980 westward a scant ½ mile. Both lakes are outstandingly scenic and have beautiful campsites. They have many delightful sand beaches, the more so since the replenishment of May 18, 1980.

From "little" Twin Sister Lake, turn left on trail No. 1104 and cross the outlet stream. In ½ mile the trail turns left toward Blankenship Meadows. Keep straight ahead on Tumac Mountain trail No. 44, which aims at the peak. The way climbs steadily in open meadows 1 mile. Note how small trees are taking over the meadowland, a phenomenon that only recently has received attention. Are the trees just now growing after the Ice Age, or are they returning after catastrophic forest fires, insect invasion, or uncontrolled stock-grazing of years ago? Whatever the reason, alpine meadows all over this portion of the Cascades are rapidly changing to forest, especially here and at Mt. Rainier.

The final mile is steep and the soft soil badly chewed up by horses, but the views get steadily better and become downright exciting on the 6340-foot summit. The most striking is northeast, down to Blankenship Meadows and the three Blankenship Lakes (Hike 24). To the west are many tree-ringed lakes, a few of which can be seen, including Dumbbell Lake (Hike 25). Mt. Aix and neighbors dominate the northeast horizon. In other directions are the volcanoes.

To protect the vegetation, campers must use sites at least 100 feet from the lakeshores. At the "larger" Twin Sister, most of the permitted camps are on the south side, one on the north.

Incidentally, don't try to puzzle out an Indian source for "Tumac." Two "Macs," probably McAllister and McCall, grazed sheep in the area.

Beargrass on top of Tumac Mountain

RATTLESNAKE MEADOWS

Round trip 20 miles	Hikable August and September
Allow 2–3 days	Backpack
High point 3800 feet	Maps: USFS William O. Douglas
Elevation gain 600 feet, plus many	Wilderness, Green Trails Old
ups and downs	Scab Mountain (No. 272)

The William O. Douglas Wilderness has a split personality: The ocean-side west, misty-lush all the way up to the Pacific Crest, and the rain-shadow east, where desert plants mingle with subalpine, the sun shines (almost) all the time, and (yes) there are (a few) rattlesnakes. The quintessence of the east is the Rattlesnake (Creek), and a person easily could spend a week ascending the stream to its source, exploring sidetrails to 7000-foot peaks. For a hiker the objections to the trail are two: The first 2-odd miles are on a jeepers' "trail" (their exclusion *must* be arranged); even so, this stretch would be a delightful early-summer walk except that at 3 miles is the first of 14 fords, ruling out the trip for the average pedestrian until the low water of August. Put on smelly old tennis shoes at the fords, and maybe they will be clean by the end of the series.

Drive SR 410 some 39 miles east of Chinook Pass, and between mileposts 108 and 109 go right on the second of the two "Niles Roads"; or, drive west from Naches about 12 miles and go left on the first Niles Road. In 1.4 miles (just before a cement bridge), turn left on road No. 1500. Stay on it, and beware of misleading sideroads. At 11 miles from the highway, pass the dramatic Mt. Aix viewpoint and in exactly 1 more mile turn right on road No. (1500)620 for 0.7 mile to the road-end and trail No. 1114, elevation 3100 feet.

Hike about ¼ mile and join a jeep track at the crossing of Three Stream. Go steeply up and then down. At 1 mile the way comes to Rattlesnake Creek, where camping would be bliss were it not for the jockeys on two, three, four, and six wheels.

A last mile of jeep road leads to the wilderness boundary (which *must*

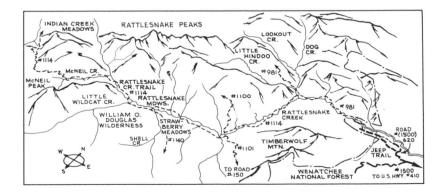

Rattlesnake Creek

be extended down the valley) and the start of true, quiet trail. But then, shortly beyond, at 2¼ miles, is that fearsome first ford, knee-deep even in low water. By late August or so, however, the wading is stimulating yet not perilous. As for the rest of the fords, none quite so menacing, some years they can be avoided by following game traces along the streambed.

At 4½ miles is a junction. The right fork is an arduous climb to Justice Douglas' favorite, Hindoo Valley, a trip on its own. To complete the Rattlesnake, however, go left on trail No. 1114, up and down steeply. At 7½ miles pass trail No. 1101, an alternate route from road No. 1500. At 9½ miles cross the Rattlesnake the fourteenth and last time near Strawberry Meadows. At 10 miles ramble into Rattlesnake Meadows, 3900 feet.

The trail continues 7 more miles to Indian Creek Meadows, well worth doing. If that is the destination, however, there are quicker routes (Hike 24).

22 CARLTON CREEK–
FISH LAKE

Round trip 7½ miles
Hiking time 5 hours
High point 4150 feet
Elevation gain 1000 feet
Hikable mid-July through
October

One day or backpack
Maps: USFS William O. Douglas
Wilderness, Green Trails
Bumping Lake (No. 271), White
Pass (No. 303)

A rough trail ascends ancient forest to the Cascade Crest, in country that is late-winter range for the elk that browse on brush in nearby clearcuts, then retire to rest in deep forest where the snow depth is less. Though there is some horse damage, it's mainly the elk that churn the trail to mud, exposing tree roots that grab for the hiker's ankles, making for slow and careworn going. The best walking is in late summer and fall when the mud has dried; the roots are still there.

Drive either US 410 to Cayuse Pass and go south on SR 123 or US 12 toward White Pass and take SR 123 to just 0.2 mile outside of Mount Rainier National Park. Go uphill on road No. 44 some 6.5 miles to the road-end parking area and trail No. 22, elevation 3200 feet.

Descend to a crossing of Carlton Creek where two large storm-toppled cedar logs are a perfect bridge. Proceed on an abandoned logging road, skirt a clearcut (note how the brush has been elk-nibbled), and enter virgin forest.

In about ½ mile cross a creek in sound but not sight of a spectacular waterfall. (To see it, walk upstream.) The next mile is through old-growth hemlock and fir, a company of ancient giants protected within the William O. Douglas Wilderness.

At about 2¾ miles is a campsite in the woods. At 3½ miles reach 4150-foot Carlton Pass and descend to Fish Lake and a junction with the Pa-

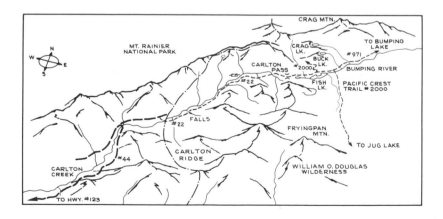

Fish Lake

cific Crest Trail, 4114 feet, 3¾ miles from the road.

Fish Lake is shallow and swampy, not the scenic climax of this hike. The forests are. For higher excitement, follow the Crest Trail north, climbing into pretty flowers and broad views.

23 FRYINGPAN LOOP

Loop trip 15 miles
Hiking time 8 hours
High point 5200 feet
Elevation gain 2000 feet
Hikable mid-July through
October

One day or backpack
Maps: USFS William O. Douglas
Wilderness, Green Trails White
Pass (No. 303)

The low-top forests of subalpine trees, intimate green meadows inter-spersed, the wildflowers and lakes and lakes, the birds and the bees and the chipmunks, are enough to fill a day. Overnight is better. The counterclockwise loop is recommended to avoid hauling a pack steeply to Jug Lake. Day-hikers can shorten the loop to 9½ miles.

Candidly, the trip has four problems: one natural, three human. *Mosquitoes:* Walk fast, carry repellent, and don't go until the frosts of September. *Signs:* Some junctions have no signs, and at some that do, the signs give only numbers. *Maps:* Some Forest Service maps do not show all the trails, and many trails are missing from the USGS maps, so a hiker must carry a weighty mass of paper. *Horses:* The cavalry rides this region in numbers approaching the squadrons of Phil Sheridan, Jeb Stuart, and the Cossacks, and where trails are wet, horses churn the soil to mud and a hiker may simply sink out of sight in black muck and nevermore be seen.

Drive US 12 east of Packwood. At the junction with SR 123 to Mt. Rainier stay on US 12 another 1.3 miles and turn left on road No. 45. In 0.3 mile turn left on road No. 4510. At 4.5 miles from the highway turn right on Soda Springs Campground Road to its end in 5 miles, elevation 3200 feet.

At the far end of the campground, set out on Cowlitz trail No. 44. In 2½ miles intersect Jug Lake Trail. Go straight ahead, staying on No. 44, to a junction at 4 miles of trail Nos. 45 and 46. For the shorter day hike, saving about 3 miles, take No. 45. Mosquito-undaunted backpackers proceed

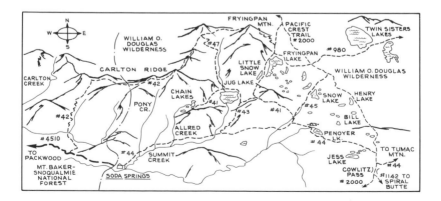

on No. 44 to Penoyer Lake, 5000 feet, 4¾ miles, and splendid camping (when the frost is in the huckleberries).

For the next stage of the loop, continue 1 mile on No. 44 to the Pacific Crest Trail, 5191 feet, 5¾ miles from the road. Turn north on the Crest Trail, gently up and down, passing numerous lakes and ponds and marshes, 2 miles to a junction on the left with trail No. 45, the shorter route. A short distance farther is a second junction. The right, trail No. 980, goes a near-level 1½ miles to Twin Sisters Lakes (Hike 20); the left, an abandoned trail, goes directly to Fryingpan Lake. Continue on the Crest Trail 1 more mile and turn left on Jug Lake trail No. 43.

In ½ mile pass Fryingpan Lake amid large meadows, continue on past long and narrow little Snow Lake and lose 400 feet to a ¼-mile spur path to ever-popular Jug Lake, 4416 feet, 2 miles from the Crest Trail.

Beyond the spur, No. 43 levels briefly and plunges 400 feet to the Cowlitz Trail, which returns the looper 2 miles to the start, completing the 15 miles.

Small pond near Fryingpan Lake

24   INDIAN CREEK– BLANKENSHIP LAKES

**Round trip to Blankenship Lakes
12 miles
Hiking time 6 hours
High point 5200 feet
Elevation gain 2000 feet in, 200
feet out**

**Hikable mid-July through
October
One day or backpack
Maps: USFS William O. Douglas
Wilderness, Green Trails White
Pass (No. 303)**

Pocket-size meadows, vast grasslands, and beautiful mountain lakes make this country unique in the Cascades. The map calls the area "Mosquito Valley," and rightly so. Though the meadows are magnificent when bright green, the bugs are then numbered in the billions; the hike is much more enjoyable in late summer and fall.

To encourage hikers to carry a map and know where they are, trails are signed only by their numbers and not their destinations, so one must carry a Green Trails map or a Forest Service map—a good system but guaranteed to confuse and lose anyone who forgets his map.

Drive US 12 east from White Pass 8.3 miles. A few hundred feet before Indian Creek Campground, turn left on road No. 1308. Drive past summer homes and at a junction in 0.8 mile keep left, still on road No. 1308;

Blankenship Lake and Tumac Mountain

at 2.8 miles from the highway is the parking lot by the trailhead signed "Indian Creek trail, No. 1105," elevation 3400 feet.

The first 2 miles of trail are an old mining road, now closed because ¼ mile from the start it enters the William O. Douglas Wilderness. Just before the end of the road, find the start of true trail, which drops steeply 200 feet into a canyon, crosses Indian Creek, and climbs very steeply out of the canyon. At about 2½ miles listen for a waterfall to the right; the canyon edge and a view of the lovely falls are just a few feet off the path, though one may have to try a couple of spots before finding the only really good vantage point.

The trail crosses Indian Creek again at about 3 miles, recrosses at 4 miles, and at 4½ miles enters the large (½-mile-long) Indian Creek Meadows. Stay on trail No. 1105, passing trail No. 1148 to Pear and Apple Lakes. The tread is faint as it traverses the meadow and heads west but becomes distinct again beyond the grass. At 5 miles pass trail No. 1148 to Apple Lake, and at just under 6 miles take a short sidetrail to the first of the three Blankenship Lakes, 5200 feet, a fair spot for a basecamp.

The first thing to do is explore the other two lakes, a stone's throw from each other below 6340-foot Tumac Mountain, a small volcano.

Another ½ mile along trail No. 1105 are Blankenship Meadows—many little clearings and one huge expanse. There are strangely few flowers in the meadows, but beargrass and lupine grow in the woods, and bog orchids and elephantheads in wet places. (Blankenship Meadows can also be reached by a 4-mile hike from road No. 1808 starting at the Deep Creek horse camp [Hike 20].)

A 3-mile sidetrip to Pear and Apple Lakes is a must. This can be done as a one-way walk, going first to shallow Apple Lake on trail No. 1148, then continuing on the same trail to deep Pear Lake, and returning to the main route on trail No. 1148.

Good camps are at Indian Creek Meadows, Blankenship Lakes, and Pear Lake. To preserve the vegetation, camp at least 100 feet from the lakeshores.

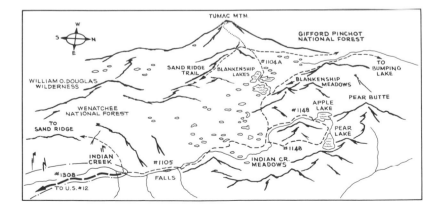

$\underline{25}$ SAND AND DUMBBELL LAKES

Round trip to Sand Lake 6 miles
Hiking time 4 hours
High point 5295 feet
Elevation gain 900 feet
Hikable mid-July through
November
One day
Maps: USFS William O. Douglas
Wilderness, Green Trails White
Pass (No. 303)

Round trip to Dumbbell Lake 13
miles
Hiking time 7 hours
High point 5600 feet
Elevation gain 1200 feet in, 500
feet out
Hikable mid-July through
November
One day or backpack

If you like serene subalpine lakes, this is certainly the trail—there are dozens of them, large and small. If you like tall, photoworthy subalpine trees, this is the trail—there are thousands of lovely specimens. And if you like fall hiking through the bright red leaves of huckleberry bushes, this is the trail—there are miles of color. The hike along a delightful section of the Pacific Crest Trail can be done as a day trip to Sand Lake or an overnight to Dumbbell Lake. But don't expect solitude. Even on a rainy day these trails are busy.

Drive US 12 east from White Pass 0.7 mile, turn left into White Pass Campground, and continue about 0.25 mile to the trailhead near Leech Lake, elevation 4412 feet. This is Pacific Crest trail No. 2000. A system of signing the authors find confusing gives trail numbers rather than destinations. There is no problem as long as a party stays on the Crest Trail, but any deviation requires a Green Trails or Forest Service map to decipher the signs.

The trail starts in forest, climbing 800 feet in 2¾ miles to Deer Lake, 5206 feet, still in woods. At 3½ miles is Sand Lake, 5295 feet, numerous

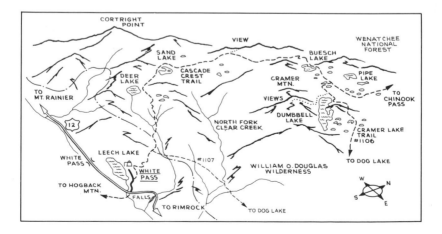

Fog blowing over Sand Lake

arms reaching into meadows and forest. Though the water is very clear, the shallow lake seems to have neither inlet nor outlet. Sand Lake is an excellent turnaround for day-hikers. (Many a person who long had wondered why the lakes hereabouts are so sandy understood after St. Helens lost its head.)

Now the trail wanders past numerous small lakes, climbing to 5600 feet at 4 miles. Several places offer glimpses southward of Mt. Adams and the Goat Rocks; Spiral Butte can be seen through the trees to the east.

At about 5 miles the trail switches from the east side of the crest to the west and descends in forest, losing 500 feet in ¾ mile. Now and then Mt. Rainier can be partly viewed through trees; for a better look, walk off the trail 100 feet onto a low, rocky knoll located on the left side of the path soon after passing two small ponds.

At 6 miles the way skirts Buesch Lake, 5081 feet, and reaches a junction with Cramer Lake trail No. 1106. Follow this a scant ¼ mile to Dumbbell Lake, 5091 feet. Much of the lake is shallow; the rocky shoreline is very interesting. To appreciate its unusual shape, beat through a patch of brush and scramble to the bald summit of 5992-foot Cramer Mountain—and views much broader than merely the lake.

For an alternate return, follow Cramer Lake trail No. 1106 down to within ½ mile of Dog Lake, turn west on Dark Meadow trail No. 1107, and finish with a last mile on the Crest Trail. The distance is about the same but most of the way is in forest.

To preserve vegetation, one must camp at least 100 feet from lakeshores. Be careful walking by the lakes. The Forest Service, with volunteer help, has revegetated some of the badly battered lakeshores.

26 BEAR CREEK MOUNTAIN

Round trip 7 miles
Hiking time 4 hours
High point 7336 feet
Elevation gain 1400 feet
Hikable mid-July through mid-
  October

One day or backpack
Maps: USFS Goat Rocks
  Wilderness, Green Trails White
  Pass (No.303)

Amble through flowers and lawns and subalpine trees on slopes of a high ridge. Then shift down and ascend lava rocks of the old Goat Rocks Volcano to the summit of Bear Creek Mountain, 7335 feet, onetime site of a fire lookout with fabulous views up and down the Cascades.

When the St. Helens cannon went off, it was pointed right at this spot; a month later the surveyor climbed from Conrad Meadows in gray ash that was inches thick atop the snow. Wind, water, and gravity are mingling the Event of 1980 with the many prior Events, but for years the hiker will find stretches of soft "beach."

The flowers are at their best in July and early August, which is nice timing, because the road to the trailhead usually is snowbound until early July; if visiting before then, approach from Conrad Meadows (Hike 27).

Drive US 12 some 9 miles east of White Pass and before reaching Rimrock Reservoir turn right on the paved road signed "Tieton Road" and "Clear Lake." At 3.2 miles cross North Fork Tieton River, and at 6.8 miles turn right on gravel road No. 1204; be careful to stick with this road. At about 11 miles is an unmarked junction; go right (uphill) on nongravel and maybe rough and rude road. At 13 miles heave a sigh at the road-end and trailhead a few feet from the murky pond humorously called Section 3 "Lake," elevation 6000 feet.

Trail No. 1130 is a dream, traversing wildflowers and Christmas trees and creeklets and many a lovely camp. At ½ mile is a junction with trail No. 1128 from the North Fork. At 2½ miles is a junction with the trail

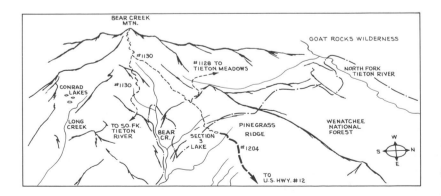

The Goat Rocks from Bear Creek Mountain

from Conrad Meadows. From here the way winds up through gaudy
rocks and cold-snowy nooks with a variety of different arrays of flowers
and still more possible camps and at 3½ miles attains the summit, elevation 7336 feet. Look out to the great volcanoes of Rainier and Adams.
Look around you, back down Pinegrass Ridge and to Devils Horns,
Tieton, Old Snowy, and Gilbert, and realize you are smack in the middle
of a volcano that was worn out and broken down millennia before St. Helens was so much as a puff of steam in a lowland swamp.

SOUTH FORK TIETON HEADWATERS BASIN

Round trip 15 miles
Allow 3 days
High point 5400 feet
Elevation gain 1500 feet
Hikable July through September

Backpack
Maps: USFS Goat Rocks
Wilderness, Green Trails White
Pass (No. 303), Walupt Lake
(No. 335)

The glaciers on 8201-foot Gilbert Peak, highest of the Goat Rocks, gleam as white as the mountain goats often seen traversing the snows. Cliffs are brilliant: the black and gray and brown of Gilbert and Moon Mountain, the yellow and red of Tieton Peak, and the brick-red of Devils Horns. Warm Lake usually is frozen until late summer. Cold Lake floats icebergs from the Conrad Glacier. All this and much more invites the off-trail explorer. Yet a hiker never need leave a broad and easy path to rejoice in grand views and sublime flowers, following the South Fork Tieton River from Conrad Meadows to its source and making a long, looping swing around the headwaters basin.

Drive US 12 east from White Pass or west from Yakima to just east of Hause Creek Campground and turn south on South Fork Tieton Road, heading westward along Rimrock Reservoir. At 4.5 miles turn left on road No. 1000, signed "Conrad Meadows," and drive 14 miles to a gate at the edge of private property. Park near here, elevation 3900 feet.

South Fork Tieton trail No. 1120 passes the gate and fords Short Creek and Long Creek to a y. Take the right, trail No. 1120, out into Conrad Meadows, the large subalpine valley-bottom meadow in the Cascades. The summer after St. Helens blew, when ash kept out the cows, the vastness of lush, table-flat greenery glowed with googols of flowers. Except in the aftermath of major eruptions, however, this Paradise is closely cropped and reekingly flopped. Additionally, in the late 1970s the spindly forests of lodgepole pine edging the meadows were logged—not for big

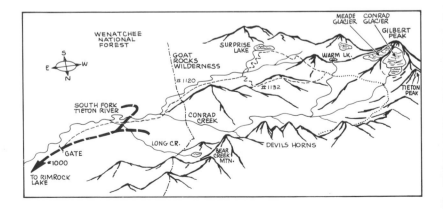

A shoulder of Gilbert Peak

Headwater basin of the South Fork Tieton River

profit (the return was nickels and dimes) but as a hobby. The entirety of the valley starting at Short Creek must be added to the Goat Rocks Wilderness.

Beware of misleading cowpaths in the meadows and gypo cat roads in the wreckage of pine forest. At 1½ miles the trail crosses the gated logging road to resumption on a route built in the late 1980s and, as of 1990, not shown on maps. The new trail goes through forest beside the South Fork, passes a sidetrail right (called the Tieton Peak Trail, though it no longer goes there), and bridges Conrad Creek close above its confluence with the South Fork. The way sidehills the ridge separating the two streams and drops to the South Fork valley floor to rejoin the old trail, alternating between meadows and woods, entering the Goat Rocks Wilderness.

At about 4 miles, 4300 feet, is a pair of junctions, new in the late 1980s and neither signed as of 1990. At the first, go right on a new path that begins an interminable series of switchbacks engineered for the heavy cavalry, climbing in deep forest nearly to the crest of the South Fork–Conrad divide. At the 5300-foot top of a small, steep meadow (all-summer trickle-creek and delightful camping), the new trail (actually, the reconstruction of an ancient trail that had vanished) commences a gloriously scenic contour around the head of the South Fork, through gardens, by snowmelt-season waterfalls, to an unmarked junction, 5500 feet, 7½ miles.

Meanwhile, at the second junction on the valley floor, the new trail leaves the old one (now abandoned), goes left to a new bridge over the South Fork, and switchbacks forest to Surprise Lake, 5255 feet, 6 miles. No backpacker of refined tastes ever would camp at this hole in the ground filled with fish and ringed by horses; continue upward a bit to the meadows and flowers and broad views and clean air of South Fork Camp. The trail proceeds onward around the basin head, at about 7½ miles reaching that unmarked junction at 5500 feet.

Junction? What appears to be a creek gully actually is the ruins of the old track ½ mile up to a 5600-foot saddle in the South Fork–Conrad divide, the start of all-direction off-trail roaming.

The new horse loop gives equestrians a marvelous ride and a camp suitable for big beasts at Surprise Lake. The Forest Service must insist that horses stay strictly to the loop. The rangers claim that there is for horses, as there is for hikers, the possibility of "no-trace camping." It is to laugh! To see the havoc wreaked in these fragile meadows, it is to weep.

For the loop, back at the junction below the saddle continue on trail No. 1120, traversing a steep hillside before switchbacking back down to the South Fork.

SHOE LAKE

Round trip 14 miles
Hiking time 7 hours
High point 6600 feet
Elevation gain 900 feet in, 400 feet out
Hikable mid-July through October
One day
Maps: USFS Goat Rocks Wilderness, Green Trails White Pass (No. 303)

Round trip from top of White Pass chairlift 8 miles
Hiking time 4 hours
High point 6600 feet
Elevation gain 2200 feet in, 600 feet out

Meadows and parklands along the Cascade Crest, grand views of the Goat Rocks and Mt. Adams, and a beautiful lake (absolutely fish-free, which is a mercy) in a green basin. All this on an easy day from the road.

Drive US 12 east from White Pass 0.7 mile to the Pacific Crest Trail parking lot and trailhead opposite Leech Lake Campground, elevation 4400 feet.

(Alternately, for a shorter hike, park at White Pass ski area, 4400 feet, climb the ski hill 1½ miles, and take a short path that intersects the Pacific Crest Trail at a point 3 miles from the trailhead described above. For an even quicker trip, some hikers ride the chairlift to the top.)

From the formal trailhead east of White Pass, the way traverses and switchbacks open forest, touching a ski run at one point, and at 3 miles, 5900 feet, intersects the ridge crest and the path from the top of the chairlift.

Now the trail ascends into gardens and scattered alpine trees on the slopes of Hogback Mountain and swings onto the west side of the crest, with a great view of Mt. Rainier. Attaining a 6400-foot saddle, the route contours steep, broad shale slopes on the east side of 6789-foot Hogback (an easy scramble from the trail to the summit) above the basin contain-

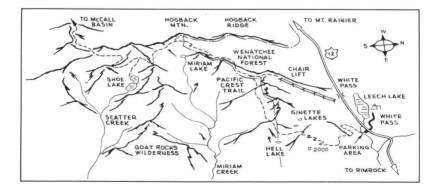

Shoe Lake

ing little Miriam Lake and climbs to a 6600-foot saddle, 6½ miles, in a spur ridge—commanding views of the Goat Rocks and Mt. Adams. And below, the bright waters of Shoe Lake.

Drop 400 feet in ⅓ mile to the lake, 6200 feet, and fields of flowers. However, due to damage by past overuse, camping has been banned in the entire basin to give meadows a chance to recover. Camping is permitted ½ mile beyond the lake at Hidden Springs. A scar of an old trail climbs the flower-covered hillside and appears to offer a delightful loop around the lake. However, as part of the healing process the route has been deliberately "put to bed" to make it unhikable.

Clear Fork trail

COWLITZ RIVER
Goat Rocks Wilderness

COWLITZ RIVER
(CLEAR FORK)

**Round trip to Camp Hagon 13
miles**
Hiking time 8 hours
High point 3700 feet
**Elevation gain 200 feet, plus many
ups and downs**

Hikable June through October
One day or backpack
**Maps: USFS Goat Rocks
Wilderness, Green Trails White
Pass (No. 303)**

Trees are the star of this show, miles of wilderness-preserved forest, and cold creeks rattling and babbling in green shadows, and a little meadow-marshy lake thrown in for the bog flowers and reeds and polliwogs. It's a scene for leisurely ambling and relaxed camping, listening to the thrushes and watching the dippers.

Drive US 12 north from Packwood 4.4 miles and turn uphill 9 miles on road No. 46 to the end, elevation 3400 feet.

Clear Fork trail No. 61 whets (dampens) the appetite with ¼ mile of jeep track through a clearcut and then enters virgin forest of Goat Rocks Wilderness. The way undulates 1¼ miles to Lily Lake, yellow pond lilies blooming in season and hordes of mosquitoes swarming, climbs a bit, and drops at 2 miles to Skeeter Shelter and a junction with trail No. 76 and Sand Lake trail No. 60; go straight ahead. The tread now deteriorates to ankle-tangling roots and the grade repeatedly rollercoasters. At 4 miles is a nice campsite beside the crossing of Coyote Creek. Chimney Creek is crossed at 5 miles. At 6½ miles, where the trail fords the Clear Fork, are fine campsites at Camp Hagon, 3600 feet.

Hikers wishing to continue can find safe logs spanning the river. An ascent of 1200 feet in 2½ miles leads to Tieton Pass and the Pacific Crest Trail.

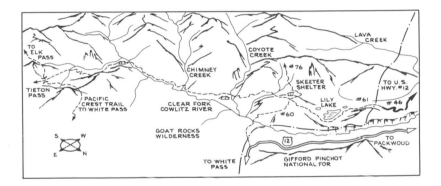

30 LOST LAKE LOOKOUT (BLUFF LAKE TRAIL)

Round trip 14 miles
Hiking time 9 hours
High point 6359 feet
Elevation gain 3400 feet
Hikable mid-July through
September

One day or backpack
Maps: USFS Goat Rocks
Wilderness, Green Trails
Packwood (No. 302)

A steep trail, generous with views, to a lookout site on the highest mountain within a 5-mile radius. Strangely, there appears to be no official name for this peak. Coal Creek Mountain could be a logical choice, after the long ridge of which it is the culmination. The unofficial name evidently was given by workers who were staying at Lost Lake while building the fire lookout in the 1930s. (The building was removed by the Forest Service in the 1960s.) Miles of alpine meadows and views of the Cascades Crest are the rewards for a grueling climb, best done with a light pack. Because the route has no water, backpackers would do better to approach via Lost Lake, as described in Hike 31.

Drive US 12 north 4.4 miles from Packwood and turn right on road No. 46. In 1.6 miles go right on road No. 4610. In another 1.5 miles, at an unmarked junction, go sharply left on road No. 4612. At 5.5 miles from the highway is Bluff Lake trail No. 65, elevation 3000 feet.

The trail enters wilderness and wastes no time gaining elevation. Fortunately, the beginning is well shaded by virgin forest. At 1½ miles pass Bluff Lake, 3800 feet, the destination of most hikers. At 2 miles the way steepens and trees thin as the trail switchbacks upward. The agony is relieved by views of Mt. Rainier, so close the crevasses can be seen in the Nisqually Glacier. The trail reaches a ridge top, enters tall trees, and with more ups and a few downs traverses near the crest. At approximately 4 miles the forest becomes more alpine, and flowers outnumber trees as the way sets out on a traverse of the Coal Creek headwaters. Across the way is 5830-foot Beargrass Butte, a good measuring stick to

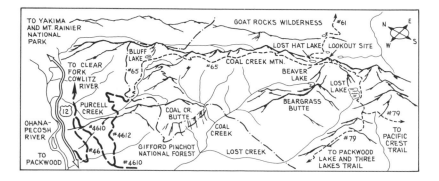

Unnamed peak, former site of Lost Lake Lookout

tell how high you are. Johnson Peak and the top of Mt. Adams are in the distance.

At 6 miles, just level with Beargrass Butte, the path crosses a large, flat meadow; sidetrip the short way for a look down to the cold basin of Lost Hat Lake, frozen most of the year, and trail No. 76 from the Clear Fork. In the next mile the trail overtops Beargrass Butte as it switchbacks up flowers and heather to the plateau summit of Lost Lake Lookout (mountain), 6359 feet, 7½ miles.

For the information of backpackers arriving from that direction: The trail continues on, descending steeply across a slippery scree slope, losing over 1000 feet in 1½ miles to Lost Lake.

LOST LAKE– THREE PEAKS TRAIL

Round trip 15 miles
Hiking time 8 hours
High point 5165 feet
Elevation gain 2100 feet in, 300
feet return

Hikable July through October
One day or backpack
Maps: USFS Goat Rocks
Wilderness, Green Trails
Packwood (No. 302)

The little lake amid meadows of lupine and lilies and paintbrush and beargrass, ringed by clusters of pointy subalpine trees, is abundant satisfaction. For more flowers—and bigger views—there is the 6359-foot site of an old lookout.

Johnson Peak from Lost Lake trail

Five trails converge on Lost Lake: Bluff Lake Trail (Hike 30) and Coyote Ridge Trail are the most scenic; trail No. 76 from the Clear Fork gains and loses a lot of elevation; and trail No. 78 from Packwood Lake is crowded. If meadows around Lost Lake is what mainly interests the hiker, these routes are not as reasonable as Three Peaks Trail. The drawback of this route is the first 2 miles are very difficult to follow weaving in and out of clearcuts, sometimes on road and sometimes on trail; stop at the Packwood Ranger Station for detailed instructions.

Drive US 12 north of Packwood Ranger Station 1.4 miles and go right on Lake Creek Road 0.8 mile and then right on road No. 1266 another 6 miles to the end of the drivable road, the beginning of Three Peaks trail No. 69, elevation about 3100 feet.

Those first 2 confusing miles are mostly steep. True trail, when it commences, moderates along crest of the narrow ridge topped by the three humps for which the trail was named. Occasional windows in the forest give views, including a glimpse of Packwood Lake. At 4 miles is a possible camp. At 5 miles enter Goat Rocks Wilderness, and at 6 miles join Packwood Lake trail No. 78 near Mosquito Lake, 4900 feet.

Go left, gently ascending a small meadow with a huge view of the giant bulk of Johnson Peak. At 7 miles pass Coyote trail No. 79, and at 7½ miles enter the flower carpet edging Lost Lake, 5165 feet. Nice camps.

If not yet overcome with pleasure, continue a steep 1½ more miles up a cliff to the flower knoll, site of the old Lost Lake Lookout, 6359 feet, offering panoramas of the Goat Rocks and other volcanoes.

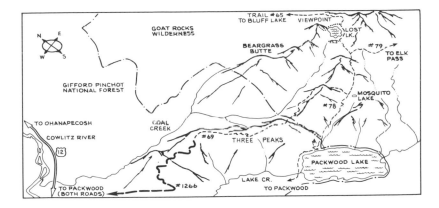

PACKWOOD LAKE

Round trip 9 miles
Hiking time 5 hours
High point 3200 feet
Elevation gain 500 feet in, 300 feet out
Hikable June through November

One day or backpack
Maps: USFS Goat Rocks Wilderness, Green Trails Packwood (No. 302)

A tree-ringed lake on the edge of the Goat Rocks Wilderness. From the outlet, look up to 7487-foot Johnson Peak. From the inlet, look back to Mt. Rainier. A wooded island punctuates the picturesque waters.

Unfortunately, man has left his mark on this scenic treasure—a potential disaster. Washington Public Power Supply System was allowed to dam the outlet to gain a small amount of "peaking" power and the Federal Power Commission mysteriously gave permission for the dam to be built 3 feet higher than specified in the agreement with the Forest Service. So far the power company has not been permitted to raise the lake above the natural level; if it ever is, the shore will be ruined.

Additionally, the trail was built so wide and flat and easy that every weekend the lake is overwhelmed by little children, old folk, motorbikers, and horsemen, all jumbled together. Though motorcyles are forbidden on the trail, they race up and down the adjoining pipeline road. Near the outlet are a small resort and a few campsites—terribly overcrowded. To avoid standing room only, visit the lake on a weekday; otherwise, pause amid the crowds to enjoy the view, then hike onward.

From Packwood, next to the Packwood Ranger Station, drive east on road No. 1260, in 6 miles coming to a steel tower and, nearby, a large parking lot and the trailhead, elevation 2700 feet.

Trail No. 78 goes gently through big trees with occasional views over the Cowlitz valley toward Rainier. As the lake is neared, the snowy, craggy Goat Rocks, dominated by Johnson Peak, can be seen at the val-

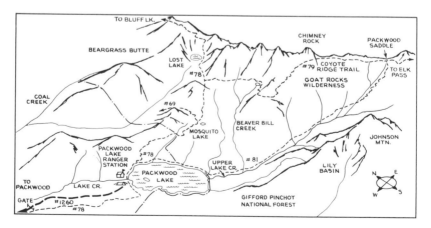

Packwood Lake and Johnson Peak

ley head. With ups and downs grossing 400 feet but netting only 167 feet, at 4½ miles the trail reaches Packwood Lake, 2867 feet. The resort and campground are across the outlet.

Some people cannot leave civilization at home and bring their radios, beer, gas lights, and noise. For quiet camping continue around the lakeshore to the inlet.

For an extra-special treat, do a 12½-mile loop from Packwood Lake. Hike to Lost Lake (Hike 31) and contour airy miles along 6700-foot Coyote Ridge on trail No. 79 to Packwood Saddle, 5520 feet. Return to Packwood Lake on Upper Lake trail No. 81. About half the distance is in steep meadows high above timberline. The way is little traveled, very odd considering the number of people at the lake and the superb scenery of the loop.

33 LILY BASIN–HEART LAKE

Round trip to viewpoint 8 miles
Hiking time 5 hours
High point 5700 feet
Elevation gain 1400 feet
Hikable late July through mid
October
One day
Maps: USFS Goat Rocks
Wilderness, Green Trails
Packwood (No. 302)

Round trip to Heart Lake 13 miles
Hiking time 8 hours
High point 6100 feet
Elevation gain 1700 feet in, 400
feet out
Backpack

Hike a forest ridge to a spectacular view of Packwood Lake and Mt. Rainier, then contour Lily Basin, a high cirque under Johnson Peak, and continue to Heart Lake and views of Mt. Adams. Logging roads to 4500 feet have ripped up the wildland and taken most of the work out of visiting this once-remote corner of the Goat Rocks.

Drive US 12 from Packwood Ranger Station west toward Randle 1.6 miles, passing the Packwood Lumber Company, and approximately opposite a small power substation turn left on road No. 48. At 8.8 miles keep right at an unmarked junction. At 9.8 miles, at another junction, turn left and stay on No. 48 another 1.2 miles to the trailhead, on the right side of the road. Park on a wide shoulder just beyond, elevation about 4300 feet.

The trail is signed "Lily Basin Trail No. 86." Climbing through timber to an old burn, at ½ mile the way enters Goat Rocks Wilderness and at 1½ miles reaches the crest of a wooded ridge, 4900 feet. The path follows ups and downs of the crest, more ups than downs, occasionally contouring around a bump. At 4 miles, 5700 feet, begin heather and flower meadows with a spectacular view of Packwood Lake and Rainier. At 4½ miles the trail dips under cliffs and regains the ridge top, proceeding to its very end at the base of Johnson Peak.

Now a mile-long contour around the head of Lily Basin leads over several creeks (the first water of the trip) and a large rockslide. At 6 miles, 6100 feet, the path tops a ridge with a magnificent view of Mt. Adams.

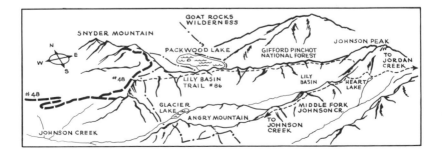

Packwood Lake and Mount Rainier from Lily Basin trail

Here, joined by the Angry Mountain Trail, it contours a steep slope and drops to Heart Lake, 5700 feet, 6½ miles, the first logical campsite.

The trip can be extended—trail No. 86 continues to Jordan Basin, Goat Lake, and Snowgrass Flat (Hike 34).

34 SNOWGRASS FLAT– GOAT RIDGE LOOP

Round trip to Snowgrass Flat 8 miles
Hiking time 5 hours
High point 5830 feet
Elevation gain 1200 feet
Hikable July through November
One day or backpack

Loop trip 13 miles
Hiking time 8 hours
High point 6500 feet
Elevation gain 1900 feet
Hikable August through September
Backpack

Maps: USFS Goat Rocks Wilderness; Green Trails Walupt Lake (No. 335), White Pass (No. 303), Packwood (No. 302), Blue Lake (No. 334)

Before the 1980 eruption of Mount St. Helens, Snowgrass Flat was one of the most famous flower meadows in the Cascades. The heaviest ashfall in an alpine area except on St. Helens itself buried the west slope of the Goat Rocks. Few flowers bloomed that summer and much of the heather was killed. Since then, paintbrush and lupine put on a spectacular show. It will be interesting to watch the meadows recover from the blast, as they have from many other blasts—and worse—over the centuries and millennia. Even were there no flowers, the constant views of Adams, St. Helens, and, of course, the Goat Rocks along the Goat Ridge loop make the trip a glory. (*Note:* The loop is often snowcovered until sometime in August.)

Drive US 12 south from Packwood 2.5 miles and turn east on Johnson Creek Road No. 21. At 15.7 miles, just past Hugo Lake, turn left on road No. 2150, signed "Chambers Lake," and at 18.5 miles turn right on road No. (2150)040, then right again on No. (2150)405 to the hikers' trailhead

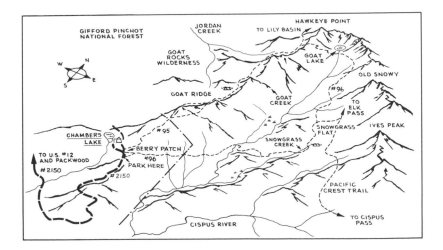

Snowgrass Flat from near Goat Lake

at Berry Patch, 21.5 miles from Packwood, elevation 4600 feet.

Set out in the woods on Snowgrass Flat trail No. 96A and soon join trail No. 96. At 1¾ miles cross Goat Creek, 4700 feet. Especially in early summer, stop at the bridge to apply insect repellent, lots of it, because here the trail enters ¼ mile of swampy forest alive with the sound of mosquitoes.

At 2 miles the trail begins climbing from the valley bottom, leaving behind the swarms of bloodsuckers. At 3½ miles reach Bypass Trail; keep left and continue up, emerging occasionally from trees into meadow patches, and at 4 miles finally enter the open expanse of Snowgrass Flat, 5830 feet.

To give nature a chance to repair the damage of grazing horses and the pounding hooves and boots, camping is no longer permitted in the Flat; however, campsites can be found along Bypass Trail only minutes below and along the first mile of trail No. 86 to Goat Lake. Either makes a fine base for exploratory walks south 2 miles along the Crest Trail to Cispus Basin and north on the Pacific Crest Trail to its 7600-foot high point on the side of Old Snowy (Hike 35).

For the loop, follow trail No. 86 northward from Snowgrass Flats, contouring a steep hillside 3 miles to Goat Lake, 6400 feet, generally frozen until sometime in August. At 3½ miles reach the 6500-foot high point of the loop and a junction with Heart Lake trail No. 86. From here the trail contours the west side of Goat Ridge 2½ miles to a junction with Jordan Creek trail No. 94 and a few feet more to a choice of trails. The left fork climbs 300 feet and traverses the 6240-foot site of Goat Ridge Lookout, the views panoramic. The right fork contours below the lookout, rejoins the lookout trail in ½ mile, and descends sharply to the starting point at the Berry Patch trailhead.

35 GOAT ROCKS CREST

One-way trip 30 miles
Allow 3–4 days
High point 7600 feet
Elevation gain 5300 feet
Hikable July through September

Backpack
Maps: USFS Goat Rocks
Wilderness, Green Trails White
Pass (No. 303), Walupt Lake
(No. 335)

Walk a rock garden between heaven and earth on a narrow, 7000-foot ridge dividing Eastern and Western Washington. This spectacular section of the Pacific Crest Trail is popular with horse-riders, so try it in the first half of July, when the tread is free enough of snow for safe hiking but not yet passable to horses; tiny alpine flowers are then in bloom, too. The climax portion can be done as a round trip of about 8 miles from Snowgrass Flat (Hike 34), but the route is described here in its full length from White Pass to Walupt Lake.

Drive to White Pass, elevation 4400 feet, and hike 7 miles south on the Pacific Crest Trail to Shoe Lake (Hike 28).

From Shoe Lake the trail crosses a low ridge and drops 900 feet into forest, and then ascends and contours to Tieton Pass, 12 miles, and a junction with the North Fork Tieton River Trail. Going only slightly up and down, the way proceeds on or near the crest to a y at 13½ miles. The left (the old Crest Trail) contours 1 mile to a dead-end in McCall Basin, 5200 feet, with overused camps and much good off-trail exploring. The right, the new Crest Trail, steeply ascends 2 long miles to Elk Pass, 6600 feet. One great compensation for the energy output is that the entire way is in open country with views of Mt. Rainier and miles of meadowland on the slopes of Coyote Ridge to the west. The last campsites for 3½ miles are in flat meadows before the final drag to the pass, at which is a junction with the Coyote Ridge Trail (Hike 32).

Views broaden at the pass—down to Packwood Lake and across the immense depth of Lake Creek to rugged Johnson Peak. The trail follows the ridge several hundred feet higher and then descends. From here one senses the quality of the route ahead. The tread can be seen—blasted out of cliffs, gouged in scree slopes; in some places the crest of the ridge has

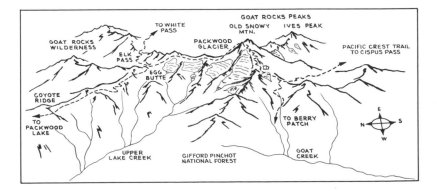

Mount Rainier and Coyote Ridge

actually been leveled off to give walking room.

The next 2 miles are mostly above 7000 feet, the highest Washington stretch of the Crest Trail and also the most dangerous. Meeting a horse party is bad business, because the horses cannot be turned around and, thus, hikers must backtrack to a safe turnout. Snowstorms can be expected in any month. Two parties have lost a member from hypothermia and there have been several narrow escapes. Don't attempt this section in poor weather.

The trail first contours and climbs to a 7100-foot point with a view of weird-shaped towers and small glaciers on 8201-foot Gilbert Peak, highest in the Goat Rocks. There is also a fine view of Old Snowy, 7930 feet. Nooks and crannies hold the superb rock gardens, which are in full bloom during early July. The way now follows ups and downs of the narrow crest, sometimes on the exact top and other times swinging around small knobs. From a spot a little beyond the lowest portion, it is possible to avoid a climb by contouring across the Packwood Glacier and rejoining the trail where several signs can be seen in a saddle on the skyline. The glacier crossing is easy in July but by late August may involve hard ice; the best plan is to stay with the trail on its ascent to the highest elevation at 7600 feet on Old Snowy, a short sidetrip scramble away from the 7930-foot summit.

The trail now descends. At 6900 feet is a rock shelter built by the Bellevue Presbyterian Church in memory of Dana May Yelverton, who died of exposure on the crest August 4, 1962. Winter snows have been hard on the building, which seems fated for early collapse.

From the cabin the path drops into parkland, at 21 miles intersecting the Snowgrass Flat trail (Hike 34), then contouring into the splendor of Cispus Basin. The route continues in meadows to the Nannie Ridge Trail at 24 miles, and then by this trail 6 miles to Walupt Lake, as described in Hike 37.

Mount Adams and Pacific Crest Trail

36 COLEMAN WEEDPATCH

Round trip 9 miles
Hiking time 6 hours
High point 5712 feet
Elevation gain 1900 feet
Hikable early July through
October

One day
Maps: USFS Goat Rocks
Wilderness, Green Trails
Walupt Lake (No. 335)

A grand viewpoint keeps the head turning around and around—from Adams to Rainier to the Goat Rocks, and down 1800 feet to tiny boats on Walupt Lake.

Drive toward Walupt Lake (Hike 37), but 3.2 miles from road No. 21— 1.4 miles shy of the lake—find Coleman Weedpatch trail No. 121, elevation 3800 feet.

The first 1½ miles ascend gently in forest, gaining a mere 400 feet. The last 1½ miles tilt, gaining 1000 feet to intersect the Pacific Crest Trail at 5200 feet, 3 miles from the road. Here, continuous forest yields to a mosaic of subalpine tree clumps and little heather—blueberry meadows, the living foreground contrasting with tree-framed glimpses of glaciers of Mt. Adams just 11 miles distant.

Turn north on the Crest Trail an easy 1½ miles to a bluff at 5712 feet. This is the place to unpack the lunch and soak in the scenery and speculate whether or not the fishermen on Walupt Lake are having any luck. Moving about the bluff gives an unrestricted view of Adams.

But, you ask, where is the promised Weedpatch? It can be spotted, a green and squishy meadow-marsh, 500 feet below, and should you descend you'll find all the weeds are flowers. However, you likely won't descend because onward from the bluff the Crest Trail is in forest, no views, for 4 miles.

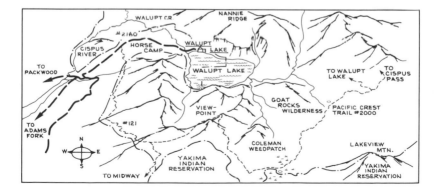

37 NANNIE RIDGE– WALUPT CREEK LOOP

Round trip to Nannie Peak 7 miles
Hiking time 4½ hours
High point 6106 feet
Elevation gain 2200 feet
Hikable July through September
One day
Maps: USFS Goat Rocks
 Wilderness, Green Trails
 Walupt Lake (No. 335)

Loop trip 15½ miles
Hiking time 9 hours
High point 5710 feet
Elevation gain 2300 feet
Hikable July through September
One day or backpack

Climb a long ridge, to views from an old lookout site on Nannie Ridge, subalpine meadows, a delightful alpine lake, and then descend to the starting point through more meadowlands to streams and ponds. The trip can be a 15½-mile loop or a 7-mile round trip to the lookout.

Drive US 12 south from Packwood 2.5 miles and turn east on Johnson Creek road No. 21. At 18.5 miles (from Packwood) turn left on road No. 2160 to Walupt Lake at 24 miles. Find the trailhead in the Walupt Lake Campground, elevation 3927 feet.

Start on trail No. 101 and in a few yards turn left on Nannie Ridge trail No. 98 and begin to climb. The first 1½ miles are in timber, passing two small streams. At about 2 miles the trees thin; the next mile is miserably rutted. At about 3 miles the way tops a 5600-foot ridge. On the very crest an unmarked, unmaintained, but quite decent trail climbs ½ mile to Nannie Peak, 6106 feet, site of a former lookout. The summit is a ¼-mile ridge of heather, grass, alpine trees, and rocks. Be sure to explore the full length—from the south end are views of Adams and St. Helens and from the north end views of Gilbert Peak and vast meadows.

Steller's jay

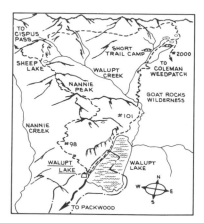

Mount Adams and Sheep Lake

Those who choose the loop now must lose a discouraging 300 feet as the main trail drops under cliffs. At 3½ miles is a pond (which may dry up in late summer) and another trail, also unmarked, switchbacking to the summit of Nannie Peak. A short bit beyond the pond look down on a small lake, about 500 feet below the trail—a tempting campsite. After passing below more cliffs of Nannie, the way regains the ridge and meadow country and follows ups and downs of the crest to a junction of the Pacific Crest Trail and lovely little Sheep Lake, 5¾ miles, 5710 feet, surrounded by grass and flowers, the camping ideal but limited. Walk around the shore for views of Adams and St. Helens.

To complete the loop, follow the Crest Trail southward, passing more campsites in ½ mile at the crossing of Walupt Creek. At 5 miles from Sheep Lake, near three little ponds, go right on Walupt Lake trail No. 101 a final 4¾ miles back to the starting point.

Mount Adams and meadow in Adams Glacier Basin

CISPUS RIVER
Mount Adams Wilderness

ADAMS CREEK MEADOWS

Round trip 8 miles
Hiking time 6 hours
High point 6840 feet
Elevation gain 2300 feet
Hikable mid-July through mid-October

One day or backpack
Maps: USFS Mt. Adams Wilderness, Green Trails Mount Adams West (No. 366), Blue Lake (No. 334)

A grand place it is to sit, gazing to Goat Rocks, Rainier, and the truncated cone of St. Helens. Green forest ridges (motheaten by clearcuts) contrast with gray ridges that lay in the mainline 1980 blast. A superb place it is to roam, among raw moraines and blocky lava flows, by ponds and waterfalls, in fields of flowers under the Forgotten Giant, the Adams Glacier tumbling a vertical mile from the summit to the edge of the gardens. A great place, too, to watch sunsets and sunrises, seas of valley clouds, swirls of storm clouds arriving from the ocean, and, at night, the monstrous skyglow of Puget Sound City. Find a campsite in the woods, please, to permit the meadows to recover from long abuse.

From the center of Randle drive the road signed "Mt. Adams" a scant 1 mile south to a split. Veer left on road No. 23, signed "Cispus Center, Mt. Adams, Trout Lake, Cispus Road." Stay on road No. 23, paved at first, then gravel, to 32 miles from Randle. Turn left on road No. 2329. In 2 miles pass the sideroad to Takhlakh Lake and at 6 miles (37.7 miles from Randle) find the parking area and trailhead, elevation 4584 feet.

Killen Creek trail No. 113 (which never goes near Killen Creek) enters the Mount Adams Wilderness, ascends open pine forest brightly flowered by beargrass in early summer, and at 2½ miles, 5840 feet, opens out in a broad meadow brilliant with shooting star, avalanche lily, and marsh marigold early on, later with paintbrush and heather, cinquefoil and phlox. Here is the first water, East Fork Adams Creek, and nice camps.

The trail ascends lava-flow steps to cross the Pacific Crest Trail, 3 miles, 6084 feet. Above the Crest Trail intersection is the uprise of a spur ridge that ultimately joins the North Cleaver, a customary route to the summit of Adams. Continue upward 1 long mile from the Crest Trail to a broad meadow swale, 6840 feet, called High Camp, Mountaineers Camp, Adams Glacier Camp, take your pick. No campfires are allowed.

The one flaw of High Camp (other than the punishment it takes in storms, evidenced by the streamlined clumps of trees) is that on any fine summer weekend it's a mob scene. But there's no need to put up with crowding. Throughout the vast meadowlands of Adams Creek Meadows on one side of the spur and Killen Meadows on the other are innumerable private nooks. Visit High Camp—and go someplace else to camp.

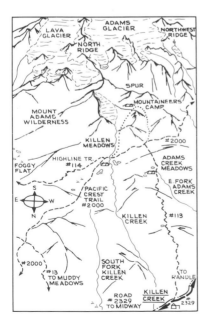

Wind-sculptured tree and Mount Rainier

39 MADCAT MEADOW

Round trip 9 miles
Hiking time 4½ hours
High point 5800 feet
Elevation gain 1400 feet
Hikable July through October

One day or backpack
Maps: USFS Mount Adams
   Wilderness, Green Trails Mount
   Adams West (No. 366)

The meadows are very nice, if small, though perhaps not as interesting as their name, "Madcat." However, the close-up views of Avalanche and White Salmon Glaciers on the southwest side of Adams and the vistas of the forested hinterland abundantly reward the energy expenditure. Morever, this is an excellent quick access to explorations high in the moraines.

Drive from Trout Lake on the road signed "Randle." In 1.2 miles turn left on road No. 23 ("Randle"), and at a sign that says it is 10 miles from Trout Lake turn right on road No. 8031. In 0.4 mile from road No. 23 go left on road No. (8031)070, pass unsigned sideroads, and beware of deep, axle-busting waterbars. At 3.1 miles from road No. 23 go right on road No. (8031070)120 and at 3.9 miles find Stagman Ridge trail No. 12, elevation 4193 feet.

The trail begins in a clearcut, enters virgin forests of Mount Adams Wilderness, and for some 1½ miles follows the long, gentle, wooded crest of Stagman Ridge, rounded on the west side, on the east an 800–1000-foot cliff to Cascade Creek. The way leaves the ridge and at about 3½ miles forks. Stagman Ridge Trail goes left ¾ mile to the Pacific Crest Trail. An unmaintained but passable (as of 1990) trail goes straight ahead a few feet to Graveyard Camp, 5700 feet. Drop a bit and contour east, still in timber with occasional windows on Adams. At 4 miles from the road is little Looking Glass Lake: Permitted campsites are 100 feet from the water. Note that on the return the trail here easily can be missed.

The trail climbs another 200 feet to Meadow Camp, 4½ miles, 5800

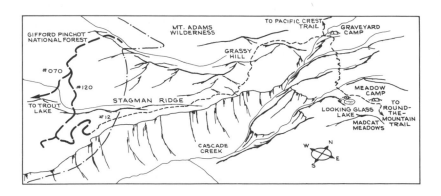

feet. Contour east several hundred feet to Madcat Meadow and views out over green (motheaten) miles of Gifford Pinchot National Forest.

Follow the trail ½ mile more to the Round-the-Mountain Trail and turn east to unobstructed views of the glaciers; a basecamp hereabouts would give time for wandering to the uppermost meadows and to moraine crests so high as to be veritable mountains in their own right. Return the way you came or by walking west to the Pacific Crest Trail, thence to Stagman Ridge Trail, and so home.

Madcat Meadow and Mount Adams

40 MOUNT ADAMS HIGHLINE

**One-way trip from Cold Springs
to Devils Gardens 24½ miles
Allow 3–4 days
High point 7760 feet
Elevation gain approximately
4000 feet**

**Hikable mid-July through
September
Maps: USFS Mount Adams
Wilderness, Green Trails Mount
Adams West (No. 366), Blue
Lake (No. 334)**

The 34-mile timberline circuit of Mt. Adams is one of the greatest highland walks in the Cascades. Foregrounds of parkland and flowers and waterfalls rise to lava jumbles that look like yesterday's eruptions to a succession of glaciers tumbling from the 12,276-foot summit. By day the hikers look out to miles of forested ridges and three other massive volcanoes. By night they gaze to megalopolitan skyglows of Puget Sound City, Yakima, and Portland.

However, you can't hardly do it. The Great Gap, the 4½ miles between Avalanche Valley and Bird Creek Meadows, has a half-dozen major glacial torrents to cross; one, the main branch of the Big Muddy, often requires a bypass high on the Klickitat Glacier. There never has been and never can be a trail—not without huge expenditures and a miles-long detour down the valley to where bridges could be built (and annually rebuilt).

Moreover, 8 miles of the circuit—including The Gap—lie in the Yakima Indian Reservation and require a permit from the Yakima Indian Tribal Council in Toppenish, a process as complicated as the Big

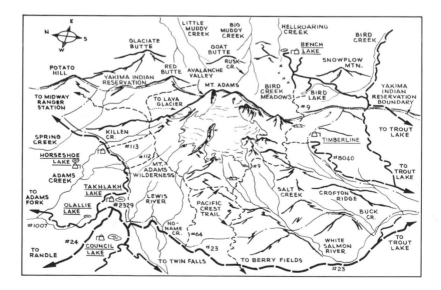

Camping near Foggy Flat, Mount Rainier in distance

Muddy. For reasons of safety and politics, we advise starting the journey not at Bird Creek Meadows, in the reservation, but at Cold Springs Campground.

From Trout Lake drive north on road No. 80, at the start signed only "Mt. Adams Recreation Area." At about 5 miles go right on road No. 8040 to Morrison Creek Horse Camp at 12 miles, and then right on No. (8040)500 to the road-end at Cold Spring Campground, elevation 5600 feet.

Hike an abandoned road, now called trail No. 183, 1 mile to the Mount Adams Wilderness and a bit more to the Mount Adams Highline (or Round-the-Mountain) trail No. 9, elevation 6200 feet.

To the right the trail contours 2 miles to the reservation boundary and legendary Bird Creek Meadows; the Yakimas allow day-use here for a fee. An off-trail, meadow-contouring mile leads to a viewpoint at 6512 feet, an overlook of Hellroaring Valley, this end of the Great Gap.

To the left the trail goes upsy-downsy, mainly in subalpine forest but

Avalanche Valley from Ridge of Wonders in the Yakima Indian Reservation

with many meadow interludes and many vistas and many tempting side-trips up to moraines and glaciers. Creeks and camps are frequent, though some of the glacial torrents are muddy, requiring the water to be settled in a pot and treated to become palatable; a little glacier milk never hurt anyone and adds body to the drink. At 7¼ miles from Cold Springs Campground, the Pacific Crest Trail is joined at Horseshoe Meadow, 5900 feet; a promontory just beyond gives a four-volcano vista, including the trip's last look at Hood.

Sidetrips continue to beckon as the Crest Trail proceeds north below little Crystal Lake and above little Sheep Lake, beyond the awesome Mutton Creek lava flow. At 14½ miles, 6100 feet, is the headwater creek of Lewis River; for a supreme basecamp, amble up the slope to meadowlands and settle down for days of exploring country below Pinnacle and Adams Glaciers. At 16 miles, 6084 feet, is a junction with Killen Creek trail No. 113 (Hike 38), 3 miles from the road; for hikers wishing to focus on Avalanche Valley this is the proper approach.

At 17 miles Killen Creek is crossed (near an overused campsite). In ¼ mile more Round-the-Mountain Trail, now called Highline trail No. 114, departs to the right from the Crest Trail, at 19½ miles entering the green of Foggy Flat, 6000 feet, a lovely meadow traversed by a clear brook. Now a stern uphill commences, from forest to the lava chaos below Lava Glacier—whose meltwater torrents may be impossible to cross—and at last, at 24½ miles tops out in the vast tundra barrens of Devils Gardens, 7760 feet. What a spot! Above are icefalls of Lyman and Wilson Glaciers, below is the volcanic vent of Red Butte. The winds they do howl up here, and the clouds do roll—though giant cairns mark the route, to attempt this saddle in a storm is to court hypothermia. Here, too, is the reservation boundary.

With necessary permits one can proceed 2 miles to the lonely wonder and sublime campsites of Avalanche Valley. What's to say about this green vale where cold springs gush from lava tubes and meander through the flowers beneath cold walls of Wilson and Rusk Glaciers, beetling crags of Battlement Ridge, Victory Ridge, The Spearhead, The Castle, and the hanging glaciers on Roosevelt Cliff? Well, when good little hikers finally check in their boots, this is where they go.

Bad little hikers spend eternity in the 4½ miles of The Gap, staggering from moraine boulder to boulder, leaping Big Muddy and Hellroaring, trying to find the one and only semi-easy way over the Ridge of Wonders, never quite attaining Bird Creek Meadows at 34 miles to complete the circuit.

Mount Adams from near Foggy Flat

41 MOUNT BELJICA AND GOAT LAKE

Round trip 8 miles including sidetrip
Hiking time 5 hours
High point 5478 feet
Elevation gain 1300 feet in, 600 feet out

Hikable mid-July through October
One day or backpack
Maps: USGS Mount Wow, Green Trails Mount Rainier West (No. 269)

On a summer day when the hikers on trails of Mount Rainier National Park outnumber the flowers, dodge away to Glacier View Wilderness. If the meadows and lakes don't quite match those in the park, the relative solitude and unsurpassed view of the mountain more than compensate. It is close enough to see crevasses in the mighty Tahoma Glacier but far enough away to appreciate the height as it tumbles from the summit ice-cap virtually to the forests.

Drive SR 706 (the way to the park's Nisqually Entrance) 3.8 miles past Ashford and turn left on Copper Creek road No. 59. At 3.4 miles from the highway keep left at a junction, at 5 miles turn right on road No. 5920, and in 6.5 miles reach Lake Christine trailhead, elevation 4400 feet.

Trail No. 249 sternly ascends a ridge, then eases to traverse a very steep sidehill to Lake Christine, 1 mile, 4802 feet. Continue past the small, meadow-ringed lake and climb a scant ½ mile to an unmarked and easy-to-miss junction. Turn left on the unmaintained trail ½ mile to the summit of 5478-foot Mt. Beljica. Anonymous until climbed in 1897 by members of the Mesler and LaWall families, the peak's name consists of the first letters of Burgon, Elizabeth, Lucy, Jessie, Isabel, Clara, and Alex.

Fill your eyes, exhaust your camera film, return to the trail, and—if

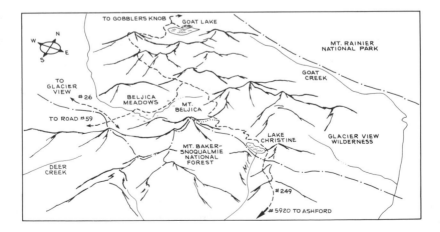

Mount Beljica

the trip is overnight—descend 600 feet more to the edge of Beljica Meadows, pass a shortcut trail to road No. 59, and at 3½ miles from the car find campsites at Goat Lake, 4342 feet.

The trail continues, and so can the trip, to Gobblers Knob in Mount Rainier National Park.

42 GLACIER VIEW AND LAKE WEST

Round trip 6 miles
Hiking time 3 hours
High point 5450 feet
Elevation gain 1100 feet
Hikable July through October

One day
Maps: USGS Mount Wow, Green
    Trails Mount Rainier West
    (No. 269)

Mount Rainier—The Mountain—perhaps must be climbed to the crater, or at least explored in the zone of glacier snouts and moraines and lava cleavers, to be fully *felt*. But it is best *seen* at something of a distance, where the neck doesn't get a crick from bending back. An old fire lookout site in a new wilderness area provides a connoisseur's perspective, superior to any in the Paradise vicinity—and on a fine summer day

Mount Rainier from site of Glacier View Lookout

having a hundredth or a thousandth of the human population. For added entertainment there are sidetrails to a pair of lakes and a lovely little meadow.

Drive Copper Creek road No. 59 (Hike 41) 7.6 miles to a ridge crossing with an outstanding view of Rainier. Continue on, going straight ahead at 8.4 miles, and at 9.1 miles reach the trailhead, elevation 4400 feet.

A short trail climbs to intersect trail No. 267, built in the 1930s to help the Forest Service protect the forests from fire, 15 miles of the trail obliterated by the road with which the Forest Service cut the forests. Trail No. 267 parallels the road a bit, often a stone's throw from clearcuts, and enters the Glacier View Wilderness at the start of a ridge extending northward.

Hardly has the hike got going when a junction presents alternatives. Save the right fork for the return, a ½-mile stroll, losing 200 feet, to Beljica Meadows, 4400 feet, a cozy marsh-meadow at the foot of Mt. Beljica (Hike 41); this trail continues to Goat Lake.

Go left, signed "Glacier View," along the ridge, with some small dips and lots of ups, swinging around the forested slopes of one of its summits and around the meadowy-rocky-woodsy slopes of another, to a saddle 2½ miles from the road. Here the trail splits. The right fork drops 600 feet in a scant mile to tiny Lake West, Lake Helen beyond, the pair worth an hour or two for collectors of lakes and fish.

The left fork proceeds ⅓ mile along a splinter of andesite to the 5450-foot summit, once the site of Glacier View Lookout. You'll understand *why* a fire lookout was here. To the west then, and the north and south, the forest view commanded hundreds of square miles of ancient giants— and now, hundreds of square miles of tiny youngsters and raw, new clearcuts at elevations so high there'll not be a second "crop" of logs until the second coming.

To the east . . . the first hour you will simply gaze. Then you'll want to get out your map and methodically identify the glaciers, notably the monster ice streams of the Puyallup and Tahoma, and Sunset Ridge and Tokaloo Rock and Success Cleaver, and Klapatche Park and St. Andrews Park. By then maybe you'll be ready to visit the flowers in Beljica Meadows.

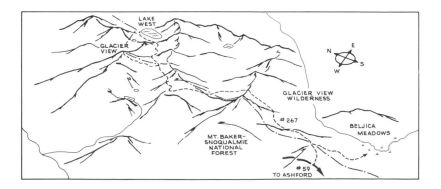

43 TATOOSH RIDGE

Round trip to viewpoint 6 miles
Hiking time 4 hours
High point 5400 feet
Elevation gain 2600 feet
Hikable July through September

One day
Maps: USFS Glacier View and
   Tatoosh Wilderness, Green
   Trails Packwood (No. 302)

A long ridge with flower meadows and a beautiful lake lies in an extension of Mount Rainier National Park, but not within the park boundary. The ridge gives views not only of The Mountain but also the backside of the Tatoosh Range, whose peaks are familiar as seen from Paradise but except for Pinnacle are difficult to recognize from here. On the highest point is the site of the Tatoosh Lookout, made famous in the 1940s by Martha Hardy's bestselling book *Tatoosh,* the story of her years as a fire lookout. (The book was reprinted in the 1980s.) The wildland vista Martha Hardy celebrated at long last has been protected by the Tatoosh Wilderness.

The trail covers the full length of the ridge, starting in the south near Packwood, climbing beside Hinkle Tinkle Creek, and ending in the north on a logging road near the park boundary. If transportation can be arranged, the entire distance can be done on one trip. It is described here from a north-end start because that way has 1000 feet less elevation gain.

From Packwood Ranger Station at the north end of Packwood, drive west on Skate Creek road No. 52. In 0.5 mile cross the Cowlitz River. (To start on the south end of the ridge, cross the bridge and turn right on Cannon Road, which eventually becomes road No. 5290. Follow this upriver 9 miles and turn right on road No. 5292 for 1.2 miles to the trailhead.) For the north end continue on Skate Creek Road 4 miles from the ranger station (sign says "3"), turn north on road No. 5270, drive 5.8 miles to a junction, and there continue ahead on No. 5272 for 1.5 miles to the trailhead, elevation 2800 feet.

Trail No. 161 sets off at a steep grade, gaining about 1800 feet, climb-

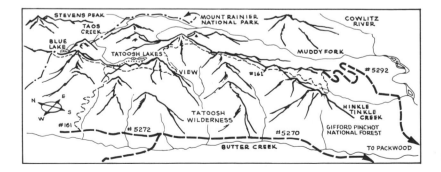

Tatoosh Lake and Mount Rainier

ing from Douglas fir forest to Alaska cedar and mountain hemlock; slopes of alpine meadows begin, covered in season with colorful blossoms. The trail makes three short switchbacks up a small stream, the only water on the main route—and maybe none here in late summer. At 2½ miles the trail reaches the crest of the ridge and a junction. The left goes to the park boundary and a possible dry campsite. Go right. Shortly beyond is a junction to Tatoosh Lakes. Proceed straight ahead but keep the junction in mind for later reference. Tread may be lost in lush greenery and soft pumice; just keep going and eventually gain a ridge shoulder, 5400 feet, and a spectacular view of Mt. Adams, St. Helens, and the Cowlitz valley. To the north Mt. Rainier looks down like a benevolent old lady, very fat.

After soaking up views, there are things to do, more to see. For one, continue on the trail 1½ miles and find the mile-long spur trail climbing to the Tatoosh Lookout site at 6310 feet, highest point on the ridge outside the park. Second, retrace steps to that junction and follow a boot-made path to Tatoosh Lakes, a small one and a large one, on the east side of Tatoosh Ridge. From the aforementioned junction, a trail of sorts switchbacks up, crosses a 5500-foot saddle, and drops to the lakes near the outlet. But the trail can be hard to follow and cliffs make cross-country tricky. No camping allowed near the lakes.

High Rock lookout

NISQUALLY RIVER
Unprotected area

HIGH ROCK

Round trip 3 miles
Hiking time 2 hours
High point 5658 feet
Elevation gain 1400 feet

Hikable June through October
One day
Maps: USGS Randle, Green Trails
Randle (No. 301)

A short but steady climb to a lookout with a breathtaking view of Mt. Rainier. The cabin sits on a point of rock that juts into the sky like the prow of a ship. Once this was a challenging hike, but now, in common with most Forest Service trails south of Rainier, it is barely an afternoon walk—or better, a morning walk, when the lighting is more striking. A good trip for small children, but hold their hands tight on the last bit to the summit. A note of caution: The Forest Service irrationally allows mountain bicycles on the steep, hazardous trail. Should you see cars at the trailhead with empty bike racks, it would be wise to go elsewhere.

Drive SR 706 east from Ashford 3.8 miles and turn right on Kernahan Road, signed "Big Creek Campground–Packwood." From this junction drive about 1 mile to a steel bridge crossing the Nisqually River. At 1.5 miles is a junction. The easiest way to the trailhead is to go right on road

No. 85 about 6 miles, then 5 miles more on No. 8440 to Towhead Gap, elevation 4301 feet. However, if sidetrips to Cora, Bertha May, or Granite Lakes are contemplated, go left on road No. 52, signed "Packwood." At 4.3 miles turn right on road No. 84, cross Big Creek, and start climbing. At 11.3 miles keep right on road No. 8400 and at 14 miles reach Towhead Gap.

Trail No. 266 starts on the north side of the gap, ascends a clearcut a few hundred feet, and enters forest. The first mile is mostly through trees, gradually thinning. The final ½ mile to the lookout is fairly open, with views to Mt. Adams and Mount St. Helens.

Climaxing all is the eye-popping panorama of Mt. Rainier. Nowhere in the national park does one get this magnificent sweep from Columbia Crest down to the Nisqually Entrance. Observe the outwash from the catastrophic 1947 flood of Kautz Creek. Note hanging ice on the Kautz Glacier. Pick out peaks of the Tatoosh Range and Mt. Wow. See the green gardens of Indian Henry's Hunting Ground. When your eye shifts from The Mountain to your feet, hang on! Cora Lake is 1500 feet below, almost in spitting distance.

At midday Rainier is a big, flat curtain of white. The best views are when the sun slants over the face of the mountain, the contrast of bright light and dark shadows delineating every ridge and valley, even the trees in the parklands and crevasses on glaciers. Therefore plan to be at the lookout before 10 in the morning or after 4 in the afternoon.

To while away the heat and flat light of midday, before or after the summit climb, visit lovely Cora Lake, reached by a ½-mile trail from road No. 8420, a spur from Big Creek road No. 84, or Bertha May and Granite Lakes, reached by a 1-mile trail from Teeley Creek road No. 8410. A very nice 3-mile trail runs along under Sawtooth Ridge, connecting the lakes, but logging roads are so close, and trail bikes so numerous, that the lakes are mobbed by noisemakers. A dirty shame.

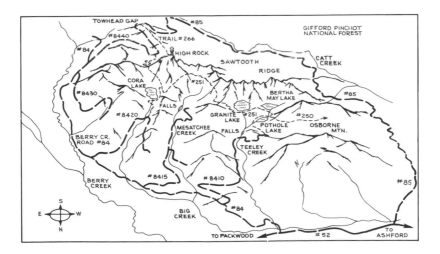

45 TRAILS END (PURCELL MOUNTAIN)

**Round trip via Purcell Mountain
Trail 16 miles**
Allow 2 days
High point 5442 feet
Elevation gain 4500 feet
Hikable July through November
One day or backpack
**Maps: USGS Randle, Green Trails
Randle (No. 301)**

**Round trip via Lookout Trail 7
miles**
**Hiking time 6 hours (unless
maintained)**
Elevation gain 2600 feet
**Hikable mid-June through
November**
One day

A basin of subalpine trees and a large flower-covered meadow, topped by 5442-foot Purcell Mountain, site of Trails End Lookout. Nothing remains except melted glass, nails, a few bits of rusty iron, a heliport, and a panorama of the South Cascades.

A few years back the Forest Service built a logging road to the 3500-foot level. Hikers complained but were ignored—or were they? Since then roading has been partly replaced by helicopter-logging, small solace for ancient forest but a small mercy for the trail system.

There are two approaches: The long Purcell Mountain Trail, which traverses the entire length of the mountain, and the Lookout Trail, which climbs directly to the summit. Snow remains on the longer route until early July, but the direct route can be hiked in mid-June with only a few snowpatches up high.

Drive US 12 east from Randle toward Packwood. For the Purcell Mountain Trail, at 5.6 miles, where the highway skirts the mountain, find the trailhead, elevation 920 feet. Park on the south side of the highway 75 yards east of the trailhead. The way crosses private land; if the owner says "No Trespassing," take the other trail, described below.

The trail starts from the valley bottom and switchbacks upward in a

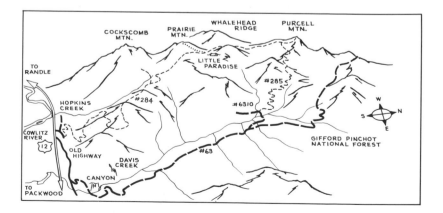

Flower fields near top of Purcell Mountain

200-year-old stand of timber, gaining 2500 feet in 3 miles. The trees provide shade but the slope faces south and has no dependable water, so carry loaded canteens. At 3 miles the trail passes "The Gate"—a local landmark, though the gate has been gone a long time—and makes a big switchback. The way is still up, but the views improve. At 3½ miles is a junction with a path to springs and open meadows, 4400 feet, under Cockscomb Mountain. Now the trail levels off, still in timber, ascending slightly under 5065-foot Prairie Mountain. At approximately 5 miles is Little Paradise, 4800 feet, a small meadow surrounded by tall trees; water and camps can be found a bit below the meadow.

What to do now? One choice is to wander the short distance up Prairie Mountain; all but the summit and steep south side are wooded. The other choice is to continue 3 more miles to the top of Purcell Mountain and the panoramas.

For the Lookout Trail, continue 0.3 mile past the Purcell Mountain trailhead, turn left on an unmarked paved road (the old highway), and in 1 mile turn left on road No. 63. In a mile look over the side of the Davis Creek bridge into a spectacular canyon. At 4.5 miles from the paved road (11.5 miles from Randle) bear left on road No. 6310, in 0.5 mile cross Davis Creek, and a short distance farther find the trailhead, elevation 2800 feet.

The route follows an abandoned road. In about ⅓ mile the trail doubles back to the right off the road and zigzags upward through a clearing, then forest. At 2½ miles the way reaches meadows. At 3 miles, 5000 feet, just before the junction with the Purcell Mountain Trail, is a possible camp. A final ½ mile climbs to the summit.

KLICKITAT TRAIL

One-way trip 21 miles
Allow 2–3 days
High point 5656 feet
Elevation gain 4000 feet
Hikable mid-July through
October

One day or backpack
Maps: USGS Tower Rock, Blue
Lake, Hamilton Buttes; Green
Trails McCoy Peak (No. 333),
Blue Lake (No. 334)

Tradition says this is part of the trail traveled by the Klickitats on trading excursions from their homes east of the Cascades, climbing from the Klickitat River to Cispus Pass (Hike 35), then descending to Puget Sound country.

But the European has come, and though the trail is lonesome, seldom is it beyond sight or sound of logging. The way is paralleled by logging roads, hacked by several clearcuts, and intersected once by a road at Jackpot Lake.

Although the trail is here described the whole length, starting at the west end, it makes more practical sense to start on road No. 20 near Jackpot Lake, exploring westward to Cispus Butte, Castle Butte, and Pompey Peak and then eastward to Horseshoe Point and St. Michael Lake. Expect snowpatches even in August

To reach the east terminus, drive Johnson Creek road No. 21 to the junction just beyond Hugo Lake (see Hike 37), go left another 0.8 mile, and then right on road No. 22 for 2 miles to the Klickitat trailhead, elevation 4400 feet. To reach the west terminus, drive 6 miles from Randle on road No. 23 then left 8.5 miles on road No. 55, then right 1.5 miles on road No. 5508, then left on No. (5508)023 a few feet and right 1.7 miles on road No. (5508)024 to the trailhead, elevation 4300 feet. For Jackpot Lake, drive US 12 east 12.7 miles from Randle (3.7 miles west of Packwood) and turn uphill on Smith Creek road No. 20 a little over 12 miles to where it intersects the east segment of the Klickitat Trail. In 0.2 more

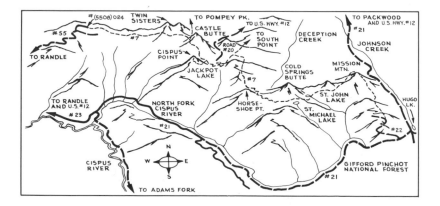

miles pass Jackpot Lake and go another 0.2 mile to the far side of a large clearcut and the unmarked west segment of the trail, elevation 4600 feet. A map is needed to figure out where road meets trail. There are some old mile markers along the route, but no indication where the counting starts.

From the west terminus, the trail climbs 500 feet, follows the ridge top, and in a bit more than 1 mile drops steeply to a clearcut. Once beyond this, the way passes under 5805-foot Twin Sisters and at about 4 miles, 5200 feet, comes to a junction with the Pompey Peak Trail.

The next 1½ miles are a glorious combination of alpine meadows and forest groves. Castle Butte towers above. At 5½ miles, an absolute must is the ½-mile sidetrip to 5656-foot Cispus Butte, the site of the old lookout with wide views of Rainier, Adams, St. Helens, Hood, and ridge upon ridge of the gigantic "tree farm" where nevermore again will trees grow to the giant size the Klickitats knew.

The trail descends into timber, dropping almost 1000 feet to the large clearcut and road No. 20 at Jackpot Lake, 6 miles, 4500 feet, and another clearcut. A traverse near the top of a 5500-foot butte has more views. At 8 miles the route drops to headwaters of Deception Creek, crosses clearcuts, and at 9 miles contours under Horseshoe Point and gradually ascends to a saddle below 5733-foot Cold Springs Butte. Along here the tread is particularly faint. The short sidetrip to the summit of the butte is well worth the effort.

The path drops through forest to campsites at St. Michael Lake, 10½ miles, 4700 feet, contours past tiny St. John Lake, climbs nearly over the top of 5683-foot Mission Mountain, and goes downward in trees, passing a junction with the Elk Peak Trail at 15¾ miles and at 17 miles reaching the east terminus on road No. 22.

Mount Rainier from Cispus Point

Tongue Mountain and Mount Rainier from Juniper Ridge

47 TONGUE MOUNTAIN

Round trip 4 miles
Hiking time 3 hours
High point 4750 feet
Elevation gain 1300 feet

Hikable late June through
September
One day
Maps: USGS Tower Rock, Green
Trails McCoy Peak (No. 333)

The Cispus River twists and turns through the forest 3300 feet beneath your toes, Rainier and Adams loom big and icy in the distance, and the perfumes of the flowers overpower the reek of your sardine sandwiches. The rocky jut of Tongue Mountain from the north end of Juniper Ridge once was the site of a fire lookout, sufficient recommendation. Juniper Peak has bigger views and more wildflowers but this hike looks straight down on the Cispus River and takes about half the time and energy, a real bargain.

Turn south in Randle, cross the Cowlitz River, and drive 1 mile. Turn left on road No. 23 and in 9 miles (from Randle) turn right on road No. 28. At 10 miles leave pavement and go straight ahead on road No. 29. In 14 miles turn left on road No. 2904 and at 18 miles from Randle find trail No. 294 on the north side of the road, elevation about 3600 feet.

Set out in second-growth forest dating from the early 1930s forest fire, gaining 500 feet in an easy up-and-down mile to a junction. The straight-ahead fork drops 5 miles to McCoy Creek; leave the motorcycles behind and go right, uphill. Short switchbacks ascend a rock garden of blue lupine and penstemon, yellow wallflower, and orange paintbrush, at 2 miles topping out in a saddle, 4750 feet. Views, flowers, the spot to open the sardine can.

The horses that used to carry supplies for the lookout cabin atop Tongue Mountain, 4838 feet, stopped here, and so should you. The footpath the final hundred feet to the summit long since has slid out, leaving a rock scramble very simple for a climber, but for a hiker, one false move and he's in the Cispus River.

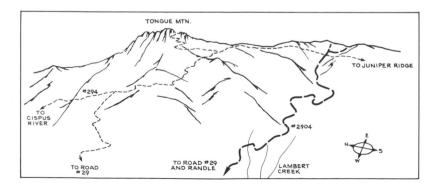

JUNIPER RIDGE

Round trip to Juniper Peak 8 miles
Hiking time 5 hours
High point 5593 feet
Elevation gain 2000 feet
Hikable mid-June through November
One day
Maps: USGS McCoy Peak, Green Trails McCoy Peak (No. 333)

Round trip to Boundary Trail 23 miles
Allow 3 days
High point about 5788 feet
Elevation gain 3100 feet in, 2300 feet out, plus sidetrips to peaks
Hikable July through October
Backpack

A classic hike with dramatic views up the Cispus River to Mt. Adams, out to Mt. Rainier and Mount St. Helens, and over endless forested hills and valleys—all while walking a long ridge, sometimes on open hillsides covered with huckleberries, sometimes in young forest just getting established after the great Cispus fires of 1902 and 1918. The route provides a variety of trips: an easy afternoon stroll to a 4500-foot saddle (the trail this far generally is free of snow in early or mid-June); a day hike to Juniper Peak; an overnight backpack; or a long approach to the Boundary Trail. Except for snowpatches in early July, the ridge is dry, ruling out backpacking. For this reason the four high points are also described as day hikes to Tongue Mountain (Hike 47), Sunrise Peak Hike—Jumbo's Shoulder (Hike 49), and Juniper Peak, here. Nearby wilderness areas of Indian Heaven, Goat Rocks, and Mt. Adams are so overused that the Forest Service is encouraging hikers to go elsewhere. Juniper Ridge offers one of the best substitutes, except motorcycles are allowed on the trail

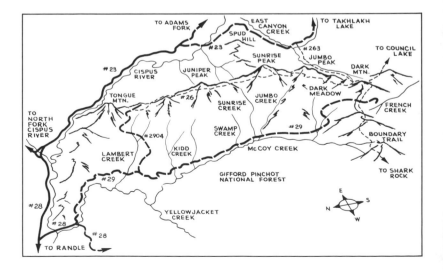

Mount Adams from Juniper Ridge

and few hikers will put up with the machines.

Drive to the Juniper Peak–Tongue Mountain trailhead (Hike 47), elevation 3600 feet.

The trail goes a few hundred feet through a clearcut, enters second-growth forest, and climbs under two prominent knolls, ascending steadily, in frequent views, 2¼ miles to a 4500-foot saddle. The trail continues climbing, gaining 1100 feet to within a few feet of the top of 5593-foot Juniper Peak and views far and near, 4 miles and a good turnaround for day-hikers.

For the full length, continue southward, dropping about 400 feet to pass beneath cliffs. At 5½ miles is a super-great huckleberry patch—outstanding even in an area famous for huckleberries. At 5¾ miles pass a tiny lake, dry in summer, and campsites.

At 7 miles is the Sunrise Peak Trail, a ¼-mile sidetrip up to the 5880-foot site of a former lookout (Hike 49). At 7¾ miles, after losing almost 1000 feet to a broad saddle, is Old Cow Camp *without water*. The trail again climbs, passing beneath cliffs of 5788-foot Jumbo Peak, 9 miles (Hike 49), and descends to the Boundary Trail at Dark Meadows, 12 miles, 4300 feet; campsites here possibly with water. From Dark Meadows the Boundary Trail leads in 2 miles to road No. 29 at McCoy Pass.

Note the many sawn stumps along the ridge to Juniper. These are not from logging but the cutting of snags, which in the philosophy of the old forestry had to be eliminated lest they attract lightning and flame like a torch. The new forestry teaches that snags are the feeding and nesting headquarters of many important birds, as well as the beings lower on the food chain that feed them, and ultimately those of us at the top of the food chain.

49 SUNRISE PEAK– JUMBO'S SHOULDER

Round trip to Sunrise Peak 4½ miles
Hiking time 3 hours
High point 5892 feet
Elevation gain 1600 feet
Hikable July through October
One day
Maps: USGS McCoy Peak, Green Trails McCoy Peak (No. 333), Blue Lake (No. 334)

Round trip to Jumbo's Shoulder 7 miles
Hiking time 4 miles
High point 5500 feet
Elevation gain 1600 feet in, 400 feet out

Walk miles of subalpine meadows aglow with wildflowers and, in season, blueberries, to a 5500-foot high point on famous Juniper Ridge, or huff and puff a steep trail to a climax of the ridge, the site of a 1930s fire lookout, and revel in more fields of flowers. Both trips give views north and south to St. Helens, Hood, Adams, and Rainier. The two can be done in a day but both cry out for a slow pace, probably meaning two trips.

Turn south in Randle on road No. 23/25, cross the Cowlitz River, and drive 1 mile. Turn left on road No. 23 and drive 19 miles to the junction with road No. 21. Stay right on road No. 23 another 4.6 miles and go right on road No. 2324. At 4.2 miles from road No. 23, at an unmarked junction, go sharply right. In another mile go left on road No. (2324)063. At 5.6 miles from road No. 23 find Sunrise Peak trail No. 262, elevation 4300 feet. (Motorcyclists are allowed on the Sunrise Peak trail, but they prefer the faster straight stretches of the ridge trail, and are seldom seen here.)

The trail crosses a clearcut and climbs steeply up in forest, at ½ mile breaking out to meadows and views of Mt. Adams and Mt. Rainier. The way follows the ridge a short bit and then traverses the slope to a junction at 5000 feet, 1 mile from the road. For Jumbo, go straight ahead, as

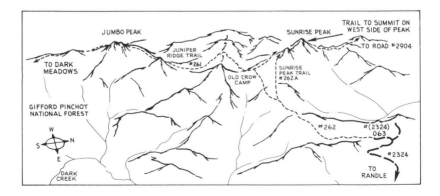

Jumbo Peak from Juniper Ridge trail

described below. For Sunrise Peak, turn right, climbing very steeply up the south side of the peak, crossing to the west side, and returning to the south side, where switchbacks attain the summit rocks. Using the lookout's iron handrail for a grip, the last 30 feet are an easy scramble to the summit, 5892 feet, 2½ miles.

For Jumbo's Shoulder, back at the junction go straight ahead, losing 300 feet, and at 1½ miles joining Juniper Ridge trail No. 261. Go left into the saddle of Old Cow Camp; no campsites and no water, so don't stop. The tread, deeply rutted by motorcycles, climbs 200 feet, rounds a ridge, contours headwaters of Jumbo Creek, and ascends more severe ruts to a large basin. The way levels off and climbs across a snowbank, which may last through July, to Jumbo's Shoulder, 5500 feet, 3½ miles from the road. Until the snow is gone and water dries up, campsites can be found in the basin. The summit of 5801-foot Jumbo Peak is only 300 feet higher, attained by a very steep, obscure trail; near the top, stay on the west side of the ridge, away from cliffs.

50   QUARTZ CREEK

Round trip to Quartz Creek Camp
  9 miles
Hiking time 7 hours
High point 2500 feet
Elevation gain 500 feet, plus
  innumerable ups and downs

Hikable June through November
One day or backpack
Maps: USGS Quartz Creek, Green
  Trails Lone Butte (No. 365)

Trees 3 and 4 feet in diameter, and even 8, line the trail, rising straight without a limb for 100 feet, a magnificent example of an increasingly rare ecosystem—the ancient lowland forest. These are probably among the best sawlogs remaining in Gifford Pinchot National Forest. The creek usually is out of sight in a deep canyon but never out of sound. Three stream crossings add excitement.

From Pine Creek Information Center at the north end of Swift Reservoir, drive 17.5 miles up Lewis River road No. 90 to the Quartz Creek bridge and trail No. 5, elevation 1800 feet.

The trail is seldom level, repeatedly climbing steeply over obstacles and dropping just as steeply. The first ⅔ mile is along the river on an old miners' road, the trees here as yet unmolested. Above the trail, just before dropping into Platinum Creek, is the old miners' rusted machinery. Platinum Creek is the first interesting stream crossing, difficult when the water is high.

The way climbs steeply, traverses a clearcut (credit is due the Forest Service for keeping the trail open during cutting operations and, when necessary, rebuilding it), and at 2 miles comes to Straight Creek. A large log with ax-flattened top spans the flood; a nervous person might feel better scooting across in a sitting position. On the far side is a good camp and just downstream are Quartz Creek Falls; other falls are upstream on Straight Creek.

The trail ascends a clearcut and at 2½ miles reenters forest, coming at 4 miles to Snagtooth Creek, another log bridge, and more camps. At 4½ miles is an unsigned junction. The main trail, marked by two blazes, goes left, uphill. Take the right, marked by four slash-line blazes, and drop ¼ mile to delightful Quartz Creek Camp, surrounded by magnificent trees,

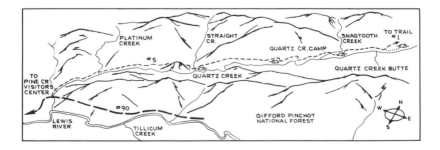

Giant trees along Quartz Creek trail

elevation 2300 feet.

Although it lacks the same loving care, Quartz Creek Trail continues. At 6 miles is a junction with the Snagtooth Mountain Trail leading to road No. 9341. At 10½ miles the way intersects Boundary trail No. 1 near road No. 2325.

51 LEWIS RIVER

One-way trip 11 miles
Hiking time 6 hours
High point 1600 feet
Elevation gain 1000 feet upstream,
    400 feet downstream

Hikable March through
    November
One day or backpack
Maps: USGS Burnt Peak, Spencer
    Butte; Green Trails Lone Butte
    (No. 365)

Huge firs, cedars, and maples serve as canopy to an understory of shrubs and a forest-floor carpet of Oregon grape, vanilla leaf, and oxalis-sprinkled moss. The Forest Service has proposed this section for a "wild and scenic" designation to preserve in a natural condition a wide corridor along the Lewis River and this trail, one of only three such low-elevation valley paths surviving in Gifford Pinchot National Forest; this 11-mile sample would serve as a poignant reminder of the hundreds and hundreds of miles of such splendor that we inherited and in the past few decades have squandered.

The trail can be hiked in either direction. Parties that can arrange transportation to allow a one-way trip would be well advised to start at the top, which is 400 feet higher than the bottom. However, parties making a round trip should start at the bottom and, thus, be sure to cover at least the lower 3 miles, location of the best trees; for this reason the bottom-to-top direction is described here.

Drive either road No. 25 from Randle or road No. 90 from Cougar. At the north end of Swift Reservoir, just past the Pine Creek Information Center, keep to road No. 90 for 5.2 miles. Turn left on road No. 9039 for 1 mile to the Lewis River bridge. Park here and find the lower trailhead across the bridge, elevation about 1100 feet.

To reach the upper trailhead, from the junction of road Nos. 90 and 9093 continue on No. 90 to a concrete bridge over the Lewis River at 14.5 miles from the information center. A few yards from the west end of the

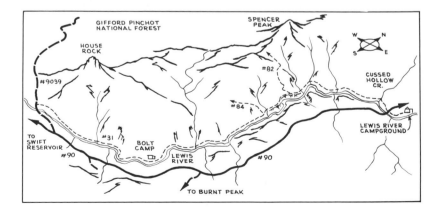

Lewis River near Bolt Camp

bridge find the trailhead, elevation about 1400 feet.

From the lower beginning, cross the bridge and find trail No. 31 on the upstream end of the road. Enter the magnificent forest. The way winds along bottomland flats, climbs a small bench, and emerges into an old clearcut at 1 mile. To somewhat beyond 1½ miles, the path follows the margin of the logging before reentering virgin trees. After a few steep ups and downs, at just under 2½ miles is Bolt Camp; the shelter here is amazingly well preserved considering it was built in the early 1930s. (In 1979 a Forest Service employee spent his days off reshaking the cabin.) At 4 miles the valley narrows to a canyon, a good turnaround for round-trip hikers, because from this point the trail goes up and down a lot but never again reaches river level.

At 7 miles the trail climbs a 300-foot bluff. At 7½ miles find a viewpoint a few feet off the tread and look down to the canyon sliced in columnar basalt. From here on the river is unseen. At 9 miles cross Cussed Hollow and climb over the last bump to the upper trailhead and road No. 90 at 9½ miles, 1400 feet.

The Lewis River Trail crosses the highway and goes another 5½ miles to Quartz Creek Trail (Hike 50), passing five waterfalls as it travels between the river and the road.

Blue Lake and Mount Adams

LEWIS RIVER
Dark Divide—Unprotected area

 52   # CRAGGY PEAK

Round trip to Boundary Trail 13 miles
Hiking time 5 hours
High point 5300 feet
Elevation gain 1700 feet
Hikable mid-July through early November

One day or backpack
Maps: USGS Spencer Butte, Quartz Creek, McCoy Peak; Green Trails Lone Butte (No. 365), McCoy Peak (No. 333)

Follow a wooded ridge to a mountain lake, 2 miles of alpine meadows, and views, and views, and views. Try this trip early in July; if conditions are right, there may be miles of beargrass in bloom.

The trail is harassed by machines and jeopardized by logging, including a timber sale ¼ mile from Blue Lake. Logging at these high elevations is particularly shocking because the timber has relatively little commercial value—a quarter or more of the trees are left on the ground to rot after being cut and a new forest may be 200 years or more growing.

From Pine Creek Information Center at the north end of Swift Reservoir, drive north on road No. 25. At 5.6 miles, at the first switchback after leaving the Muddy River, turn right on road No. 93. Watch all intersections carefully; during logging operations some sideroads are used more than the main road. At 18.7 miles the pavement ends. Go left on road No. 9327 another 0.3 mile to Craggy Peak trail No. 3, elevation 3600 feet.

The trail crosses clearcuts and at one point is only ½ mile from road No. 9331 (the road is gated). At 2½ miles pass close to a clearcut, which could be used as a shortcut; to reach this alternative starting point, walk road No. 9331 about 1⅓ miles and go left on an unmarked spur.

In the next 2 miles the trail climbs gently, eventually ascending a wide ridge. At a little over 4 miles, the ridge becomes quite narrow and at times the hillside is steep. But the vista begins. At 5200 feet the way contours around a high point at 4½ miles. The timber thins, the trail enters meadows. At 5 miles, 5200 feet, is a spring and a possible campsite. For better sites find a way trail descending 400 feet to Basin Camp. Or better yet, go all the way down to Blue Lake at 4553 feet. (This also can be reached by walking road No. 9331 some 2½ miles and finding a path of sorts to the lake.)

The Craggy Peak Trail continues crossing over a 5300-foot high point and contours under the green slopes of Craggy Peak to join the Boundary Trail, elevation 5100 feet, 6 miles from the trailhead.

As seen from the trail, Shark Rock, at the head of Clear Creek, is the most impressive hunk of rock on the Dark Divide. For widest views, take a faint boot-beaten path up the east ridge to the top of 5725-foot Craggy Peak.

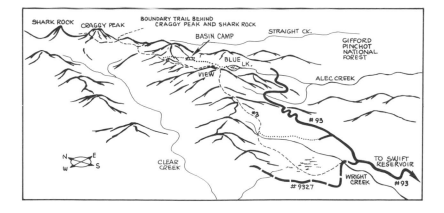

BADGER PEAK

Round trip 10 miles
Hiking time 7 hours
High point 5664 feet
Elevation gain 1600 feet

Hikable late July through
** September**
One day or backpack
Maps: USGS French Butte, Green
** Trails McCoy Peak (No. 333)**

The Forest Service blasted off the top of the peak to make a flat space for a fire-lookout cabin. The cabin is gone, along with a lot of the forests it was there to help protect, but the views haven't quit. South is Mt. Hood, east are Mt. Adams and jagged crags of Shark Rock Scenic Area, north is Mt. Rainier, and west is a close-up look of the smoldering remains of Mount St. Helens. However, the hike is not unmixed glee because loggers are working both sides of the route, a forested ridge. Furthermore, much of the tread is inches deep in 1980 pumice, as slow going as dry sand. Finally, hikers not equipped with ice ax and knowledge of how to use it must not attempt the peak in early summer, when a dangerous snow gully blocks the trail near the summit. This hike can also start from Mosquito Meadow trail No. 292 on road No. 28. While the distance is a bit shorter, the elevation gain is greater.

Drive road No. 25 to Elk Pass, 24 miles from Randle, 40 miles from Cougar, and find the parking area for Boundary Trail No. 1 on the west side of the highway about 200 feet north of the pass, elevation 4080 feet.

Walk across the highway and enter woods. The trail sets out along ups and downs of the ridge crest, at 2 miles passing Mosquito Meadow trail No. 292, the alternate starting point. The way ascends across ridge slopes to a junction at 4 miles, several hundred feet from Badger Lake, 4940 feet. Campsites here rely on the lake for water, to be kept in mind should you be of a mind to take a swim.

The summit of Badger Peak is a scant 1 mile from the lake. To get there, climb from the junction in soft pumice, contouring a steep slope. In

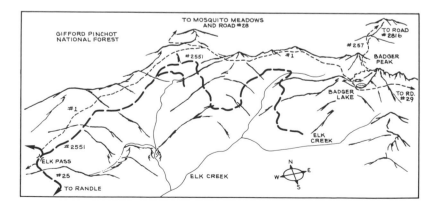

Mount Rainier from top of Badger Peak

¼ mile pass Badger Ridge trail No. 257 (from road No. 2816). (Two game traces as good as the built trail also ascend the ridge.) Just below the summit is a steep gully, unworthy of notice when snow free, but when full, one slip and you're 300 feet down the mountain, battering the boulders.

Aside from that, simply remember to beware of active volcanoes.

LAKE WAPIKI

Round trip 9 miles
Hiking time 6 hours
High point 5685 feet
Elevation gain 1700 feet in, 500 feet out
Hikable late July through October

One day or backpack
Maps: USFS Indian Heaven Wilderness, Green Trails Lone Butte (No. 365), Mount Adams West (No. 366)

Every hiker of Indian Heaven has a favorite trip. Some like to immerse themselves in bushels of lakes, as in Hike 55. Others home in on a single choice spot, such as Placid Lake or Junction Lake. But all connoisseurs agree that Lake Wapiki, walled by cliffs on three sides, 5925-foot Lemei Rock towering above, is outstanding. The route described here throws in high viewpoints and wildflowers; the hiker not interested in these can use a slightly shorter access from road No. 24.

For the 7-mile short round-trip way, minus the wildflowers and views, from Cultus Creek Horse Campground drive east to Little Goose Campground and hike the Filloon Trail, then Lemei trail No. 34, and finally trail No. 34A to the lake.

By driving road No. 24 to Indian Berry Fields, Cultus Creek Campground can be reached from Carson City or Randle. The Trout Lake route described here is the shortest from a state highway. In Trout Lake drive past the Forest Service ranger station and follow signs to Berry Fields and Carson City. Within a mile the road makes a left turn and passes road No. 88. Stay on the Carson City road, which becomes forest road No. 24. At about 7½ miles the Carson City road goes straight ahead and road No. 24 makes an abrupt right turn. Don't miss it, stay on No. 24. In another 6½ miles pass the Little Goose Creek Campground, the alternate starting point. At 8½ miles go left into Cultus Creek Campground. Find

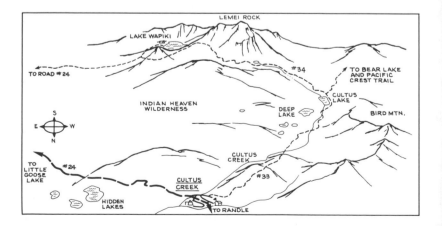

the trailhead in the back of the campground, parking space for three or four cars, elevation 3988 feet.

Begin on trail No. 33, climbing 1000 feet in 2 miles—steeply in spots—to Cultus Lake, 5100 feet. Round the shores and go left on trail No. 34, through heather, avalanche lilies, blueberries, with views of Adams and Rainier, the way climbing to a 5685-foot high point just 250 feet below the summit cliffs of Lemei Rock, and a promontory 500 feet above Lake Wapiki. To aforementioned views add Hood, beyond the Columbia River, miles and miles of forest, and, in the distance, farm fields.

The trail descends ½ mile to a junction 4 miles from Cultus Creek Campground. Go right, gaining 100 feet in ½ mile to Lake Wapiki, a great place to camp (100 feet from water)—but be aware that some hikers also think it's a great place to swim.

Lake Wapiki

55 INDIAN HEAVEN LOOP

Short loop trip 9½ miles	**One day or backpack**
Hiking time 6 hours	**Maps: USFS Indian Heaven**
High point 5237 feet	**Wilderness, Green Trails Lone**
Elevation gain 1700 feet	**Butte (No. 365), Wind River**
Hikable July through October	**(No. 397)**

A fascinating portion of the Pacific Crest Trail, with 23 lakes big enough to have names, and almost 100 smaller lakes, ponds, and tadpole pools, all in an area at about 5000 feet elevation, a mixture of forest, groves of subalpine trees, and flat, grassy meadows, the foregrounds complemented by occasional glimpses of glaciered volcanoes.

Indian Heaven has been well known to hikers and horsemen for many years, but its remoteness kept use to a minimum. In recent years logging roads have skirted the area, giving easy access to the innermost lakes and meadows. Then in 1984 Congress designated the Indian Heaven Wilderness and its fame has grown. Trappers' paths and trails built in the soft pumice by the Forest Service for the occasional use of a half-century ago were unable to withstand the increased recreational use, especially the heavy pounding by horses, which turned the soft soil into quagmires. As a solution, the Forest Service built new trails on soil that can better withstand impact and abandoned the former trail system.

However, many old maps, including the USGS maps and older Forest Sevice maps, show the old trails, and experienced hikers seeking a bit of solitude are finding them. Unfortunately, a number of solitude-loving horse people also use these unstable trails; the resource damage the Forest Service tried to eliminate continues.

The new trails can be sampled on a 1-day, 10-mile loop hike, an overnight 18-mile loop, or by spending several days in order to visit more lakes. The lakes usually melt free of snow early in July, but since Indian Heaven has been appropriately called "Mosquito Heaven," the trip is recommended for late August or September when the bugs are gone and, incidentally, the blueberries are ripe.

The starting point is Cultus Creek Campground, elevation 3988 feet,

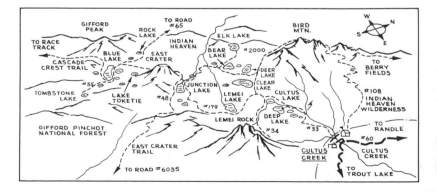

Cultus Lake and Lemei Rock

reached from Trout Lake on road No. 24 (Hike 54).

Whatever the chosen trip, start on trail No. 33, thus avoiding a very steep and hot ascent of 1200 feet on trail No. 108, which is better used for the return leg of the loop.

Trail No. 33 begins in forest, climbing 600 feet in the first mile. At 1¾ miles make the short sidetrip on trail No. 33A to Deep Lake for the view of Mt. Adams rising over treetops, then proceed to Cultus Lake at 2 miles, 5050 feet, a body of water typical of many of the lakes, having trees around half the shore, meadows around the rest. To the southeast is 5925-foot Lemei Rock and to the northwest 5706-foot Bird Mountain; one or the other of these peaks can be seen from a number of the lakes. The way climbs 100 more feet, then descends to meet Lemei Lake trail No. 179. For the short loop, keep right, staying on trail No. 33; pass within a few yards of Clear Lake, coming to the Pacific Crest Trail near Deer Lake at 4 miles. Head north on the Crest Trail, passing a sidetrail to Deer Lake and numerous ponds. At about 8 miles turn right on trail No. 108, climb over a 5237-foot saddle in Bird Mountain (a great view of Mt. Rainier), and drop steeply 1½ miles to Cultus Creek Campground.

For the longer loop that adds another 4 or more miles, along with more lakes and large meadows, from Cultus Lake follow trail No. 33 up and over a wooded saddle. In ½ mile from the lake go right on trail No. 179, passing Lemei Lake; at some 2½ miles from Cultus Lake reach Junction Lake and the Pacific Crest Trail. Turn south on the Crest Trail for a possible 2-mile (each way) sidetrip to Blue, Sahalee, and Tyee Lakes; in another 4 miles is the Indian Racetrack.

For the loop, from Junction Lake go north on the Pacific Crest Trail passing Bear Lake to intersect trail No. 33 near Deer Lake. Either return on trail No. 33 to Cultus Lake or continue on the Crest Trail to cross the Bird Mountain saddle as described above.

Don't be fooled by the seemingly flat terrain—the paths have many short ups and downs. Campsites are numerous, some by lakes and others by streams; campers must stay 100 feet from water. The pumice soil is very fragile, so camp in the forest or in already established campsites. The lakes and streams have a very small flow of water, so to avoid contamination keep the washing of dishes and bodies far away from the water's edge.

Racetrack and Mount St. Helens

WIND RIVER
Indian Heaven Wilderness

56   RACETRACK

Round trip 7 miles	**Hikable mid-July to October**
Hiking time 4 hours	**One day**
High point 4300 feet	**Maps: USGS Wind River, Green**
Elevation gain 800 feet	**Trails Wind River (No. 397)**

In 1853 naturalist George Gibbs wrote (as quoted by Harry M. Majors in *Exploring Washington*), "The racing season is the grand annual occasion of these tribes. A horse of proved reputation is a source of wealth or of ruin to his owner. On his steed he stakes his whole stud, his household goods, clothes, and finally his wives. . . . They ride with skill, reckless of all obstacles, and with little mercy to their beasts, the right hand swinging the whip at every bound. . . . The Indians ride with hair-rope knotted around under their jaw for a bridle. The men use a stuffed pad, with wooden stirrups."

The Klickitat and Yakima peoples came here in late summer to pick huckleberries and dry them in the sun. The highland then was a vast berryfield, whether because the harvesters regularly set fires to burn encroaching forests, or because the Little Ice Age had kept the treeline at lower elevations, or a combination. For centuries, perhaps millennia, they traveled (perhaps) the trails we now walk, to places suitable for combining the berry harvest with picniclike socializing. Having at some time in the eighteenth century acquired horses from neighbors (ultimately, from the Spanish in Mexico), they began to bring along their nags for the sport Gibbs observed. In the Racetrack meadow they wore a rut 2000 feet long, but only a few hundred feet can be seen, trees having invaded most of the meadow; despite modern horse-riders who like to run their mounts along it, the rut is mere inches deep. This isn't a place to see history. But if you sit a spell picking huckleberries you can feel it.

From Trout Lake drive to the Berryfields, then south on Wind River road No. 30 for some 7 miles. Go left 6.6 miles on road No. 65 to Racetrack trail No. 171, elevation 3500 feet. (From the south drive north from Carson 10 miles on Wind River Highway, go right 10.6 miles on road No. 60, signed "Carson-Guler," and turn left 5 miles on road No. 65 to the trailhead.)

In ¼ mile the trail reaches Falls Creek, the only all-summer water on this route, and in early summer too much water, the boulder-hop crossing not rationally possible. However, since the huckleberry time of September is the usual time of a hike (unless one wishes to see the acres of beargrass blooming in mid-July), the creek generally is more pleasing than repelling. For 1 mile the trail climbs rather briskly, then levels off and drops a bit to the Racetrack, 2½ miles, 4300 feet, near a pond that dries up in summer.

For the best overview of the Racetrack meadow, climb the steep Red Mountain Trail in woods to the top of the first hill, leave the trail, and ascend north on pumice slopes to a bare knoll with an aerial 4700-foot perspective 3½ miles from road No. 65.

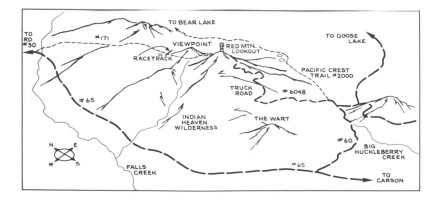

57 SHEEP CANYON LOOP

Loop trip 7 miles
Hiking time 4 hours
High point 4700 feet
Elevation gain 2400 feet
Hikable July through October

One day
Maps: USGS Mount St. Helens,
    partly on Green Trails Mount
    St. Helens (Nos. 364 and 364S)

Be properly awed and somewhat fearful, thinking what it would have been like to be here that awful Sunday in May 1980. Cross giant mudflows, pass trees that were laid flat by the 300-mph winds that accompanied the eruption, and trees that were killed by heat. Find evidence of prior eruptions. And yet, for most of the way, hike in tall trees that have escaped the many eruptions during their 300 years since seedlinghood. And explore alpine meadows with flowers as colorful as they've ever been.

From road No. 90, near the south end of Swift Reservoir, turn uphill on road No. 83 for 3 miles, then left 5 miles on road No. 81, and finally go right on road No. 8123 for 10.5 miles to the road-end trailhead, elevation 3360.

Sheep Canyon trail No. 240 climbs an easy ½ mile to Sheep Canyon, stripped of vegetation by the mudflow. At a junction go left on trail No. 238, crossing Sheep Creek on a bridge. Climb back into forest, descend 600 feet to a crossing of a stream below Crescent Ridge, approximately 2900 feet, and skirt the enormous mudflow of South Fork Toutle River to a junction with Loowit Trail No. 216, 1¾ miles from the road. Before 1980 this valley was a deep forest of 300-year-old trees; all were carried away by the turmoil of rock and water from melted glaciers. Go right on the Loowit Trail, climbing almost 2000 feet in forest with occasional views of the mudflow. Finally, reach trees killed by superheated air estimated to have been 480 degrees Fahrenheit. The way climbs flower gardens, in views of alpine meadows and snowfields of Mount St. Helens, to

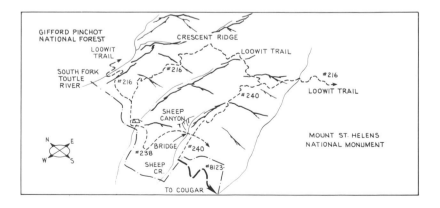

Sheep Canyon and Mount St. Helens

a 4700-foot high point about 3½ miles from the start. The way then descends into scorched forest, traversing the headwaters of Sheep Canyon. At approximately 5½ miles is the junction of Sheep Canyon trail No. 240. Either descend 2 miles back to the starting point or, if the day is still young, explore southward a mile or two along the Loowit Trail, ascending again into meadowland before backtracking and descending the Sheep Canyon Trail.

58   LOOWIT TRAIL

Loop trip 28 miles
Allow 3 days
High point 4800 feet
Elevation gain 4100 feet

Hikable mid-July through
   September
Maps: USGS Mount St. Helens,
   partly on Green Trails Mount
   St. Helens (Nos. 364 and 364S)

Circle the remains of Mount St. Helens. Marvel at how little is left to remind that it was once called the Fujiyama of the West, and that its oldest name was Loowit, for the beautiful young girl who was turned into a beautiful mountain. While the loop is only 28 miles, the trail does not touch a road, so the access trail is added to the total distance. The trail is not easy, dropping down numerous steep walls and deep into gullies, crossing fields of ankle-twisting lava blocks and pumice slopes as tiring as soft snow. Campsites with water are rare, many miles are shadeless and exposed to sun, wind, and dust storms of volcanic ash. Though the hike is strictly for the experienced, there is no better place to fully appreciate the cataclysm of May 18, 1980.

The trail is too new for the kinks to have been worked out by hiker use and a "best way" generally accepted. The seven possible starting points all have disadvantages. The rugged northern crossing of the 13-mile moonscape from Ape Canyon to South Fork Toutle River distinctly is not for the faint of heart; it is described here (but not necessarily recommended) starting at Windy Point. By use of two cars, the loop can be done in sections, saving packing over rough ground.

From road No. 25, between Randle and Cougar, drive road No. 99 some 16 miles to its end at Windy Point, elevation 4000 feet. Walk the gated service road signed "Truman Trail No. 207" toward the mountain for 2 miles, first climbing a bit, then going down to a dry wash. Leave the road here and climb 1 mile on the obscure Windy trail No. 216E to intersect

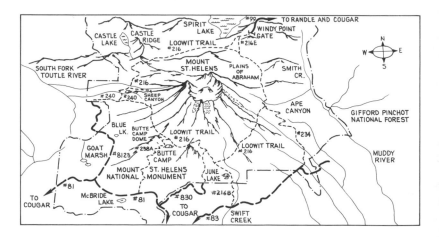

Loowit Trail crossing pumice fields on north side of Mount St. Helens

the Loowit Trail at 4500 feet. Please note: Stay with the trail; the barren pumice slopes are easily disturbed by feet. (Hikers are prohibited from wandering more than 10 feet from the trail anywhere in the Spirit Lake Basin to protect the sensitive environment and the hundreds of research plots.)

Once on the Loowit Trail, head west, in and out of numerous dry gullies. Look down on Spirit Lake, up at the gaping crater, and out to miles and miles of barren hills that were denuded by the blast in the blowdown zone that extended 14–17 miles to the west. At approximately 7 miles reach Castle Ridge and at 4000 feet join a section of Toutle trail No. 238. Keep left, dropping steeply into the loose ash of the Pumice Bowl, to a crossing of the South Fork Toutle River. A bit farther is an intersection, at about 3200 feet. For an excellent campsite follow this trail a scant ½ mile to a stream.

To continue the loop, Loowit trail No. 216 climbs out of the blast area and switchbacks up virgin forest of Crescent Ridge into scorched trees and to flower fields, attaining a 4700-foot high point at the edge of meadows. The best stretch of the trail ensues, descending into a subalpine forest. With many ups and downs, the way ascends again to timberline, and at approximately 5½ miles from the South Fork Toutle reaches a junction with Butte Camp trail No. 238A. If the hour is late, take the 1¼-mile detour and an 800-foot elevation loss to campsites at Butte Camp.

In the next 5 miles, the pace becomes slower and the routefinding tricky, the trail often obscure as it crosses lava fields, losing 1400 feet to a junction with the June Lake Trail; a ⅓-mile sidetrip leads to campsites at June Lake. The next 4¾ miles are equally difficult, traversing more cruel lava flows to a junction with the Ape Canyon Trail. The trail then improves and the remaining 4 miles across the Plains of Abraham to the final junction are generally smooth sailing. Turn right to road No. 99 (gated) and 2 miles back to the Windy Point parking lot.

59

NORWAY PASS—
MOUNT MARGARET

**Round trip to Norway Pass 5½
  miles**
Hiking time 3 hours
High point 4508 feet
Elevation gain 900 feet
Hikable July through September
One day
**Maps: USGS Spirit Lake, Green
  Trails Spirit Lake (No. 332)**

**Round trip to Mt. Margaret 11
  miles**
Hiking time 6 hours
High point 5858 feet
Elevation gain 2300 feet
**Hikable August through
  September**
One day

A stretch of the Boundary Trail provides the best vantage to feel (down to your twitching toes, eager to make a dash to safety) the devastation of May 1980, to gaze in awe at the new (and ghostly) Spirit Lake and the crater blasted from the former perfect symmetry of Mount St. Helens, the "Fujiyama of the West." Wear sturdy shoes for wading through pumice. Carry water and be prepared for hot sun—there is no shade (no trees) on the trail.

Note: The Boundary Trail crosses some steep snow slopes below Mt. Margaret that may not be safe until late summer.

There are two trailheads. For best views of Spirit Lake and the steaming crater, start from the Windy Ridge Road at Independence Pass, adding 1½ miles (each way) to the round-trip distance. However, for the

Mount St. Helens and log-covered Spirit Lake from Norway Pass

spectacular views from Mt. Margaret, it is better to start on the Boundary Trail near Meta Lake, as described here.

Drive road No. 25 either 22 miles from Randle or 44 miles from Cougar and turn uphill on road No. 99, signed "Mount St. Helens—Windy Ridge Viewpoint." At 8.9 miles from road No. 25 turn right on Ryan Lake road No. 26 and in 1 mile reach Boundary Trail/Norway Pass trailhead, elevation 3600 feet.

The trail ascends in switchbacks through blown-down timber. Note that on slopes where the blast of hot gas and ash blew straight from the mountain the trees lie flat in tidy parallel lines; where the blast eddied in the lee of a hill, they are piled one atop the other in a haphazard jackstraw.

The feature of interest near the pass used to be the old mining machinery; that all disappeared, though there is a badly dented boiler from the Camp Fire Girls' camp on Spirit Lake. The view, of course, is now the thing. Look down to Spirit Lake, half-filled with logs. Note how a giant "tidal" wave (the technically accurate term is *seiche*) washed away the forests 500 feet above the shore.

From the pass continue westward, climbing with several substantial ups and downs, into the flower gardens of Mt. Margaret and views down to the Mt. Margaret backcountry lakes—first Grizzly Lake, then Boot and Obscurity Lakes. At about 5½ miles a short spur leaves the Boundary Trail and climbs to within 20 feet of the 5858-foot summit of Mt. Margaret and aerial views of Spirit Lake and Mount St. Helens. To the north is Rainier, east Adams, and south Hood.

The Boundary Trail continues to Coldwater Peak at 10 miles. The Coldwater Peak Trail can be taken ¾ mile from the Boundary Trail to the summit. The Boundary Trail turns south, looping above St. Helens Lake along the east slope of the ridge. The way switches to the west side of the ridge through a natural rock arch, which frames a view of Mt. Adams. A descent leads to the intersection of Harry's Ridge Trail, which goes a long ½ mile to a viewpoint above Spirit Lake. The Boundary Trail proceeds to where a portion of the massive debris avalanche crossed the North Fork Toutle River, swept upward 1500 feet, and spilled over the ridge into the Coldwater drainage. Here the Boundary Trail ends and the Truman Trail begins. In 1992 the Boundary Trail will be constructed to the Johnston Ridge Volcano Observatory, scheduled to open in 1994.

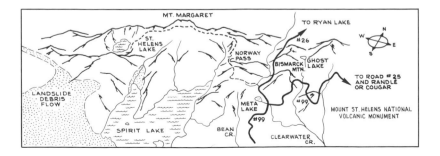

Mount Rainier and tarn on Goat Mountain

60 GOAT MOUNTAIN

Round trip to Deadmans Lake 11 miles
Hiking time 5½ hours
High point 5300 feet
Elevation gain 1900 feet in, 1000 feet out

Hikable July through mid-October
One day or backpack
Maps: USGS Spirit Lake, Green Trails Spirit Lake (No. 332)

One of the most exciting ridge walks in the South Cascades, along the 2½-mile-long crest of Goat Mountain, through meadows of soft pumice spotted with flowers, huckleberry bushes, and subalpine trees, by little spring-fed lakelets ringed by fields of grass, to ¼-mile-wide forest-ringed Deadmans Lake. Views south to the depths of the Green River valley, to the Mt. Margaret backcountry topped by Mount St. Helens, and north out Quartz Creek valley to Rainier.

Drive south from the center of Randle on the road signed "Cispus, Mt. Adams, etc." Cross the Cowlitz River and at a junction in 1 mile keep straight on road No. 25. At 8.7 miles cross the Cispus River to a junction. Continue straight ahead on road No. 26, signed "Ryan Lake." At 22.5 miles from Randle, turn right on road No. 2612 and at 22.8 miles find the trailhead, No. 217, just beyond the Ryan Lake parking area, elevation 3400 feet.

The trail begins with a ¾-mile walk over the fairly level Devastated Area, then turns steeply upward switchbacking in and out of the Blast Area, and at 1¾ miles, 4600 feet, tops the crest of Goat Mountain, which, by the chances of the eruption, escaped the catastrophe.

The way follows the ups and downs of the crest. At 2 miles the trail passes above the first of the lakelets, at 3 miles contours around a 5600-foot high point, and at 3¾ miles, 5200 feet, crosses from the south side of the ridge to the north, directly above two more lakelets. Now begins a 900-foot descent to Deadmans Lake, 5½ miles, a wonderful spot for a basecamp. The trail can be followed another 2¾ miles to 4948-foot Vanson Peak, site of a former lookout; a sidetrip leads to Vanson Lake.

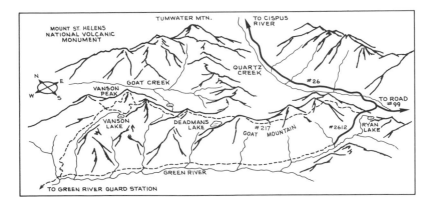

61 OBSERVATION (TRAPPER) PEAK LOOP

Loop trip from Government Mineral Spring 13 miles
Hiking time 7½ hours
High point 4207 feet
Elevation gain 2900 feet
Hikable June through September
One day
Maps: USFS Trapper Creek Wilderness, Green Trails Lookout Mountain (No. 396), Wind River (No. 397)

Round trip from road No. 58 6 miles
Hiking time 3 hours
High point 4207 feet
Elevation gain 1600 feet in, 300 feet out

A loop trip through forest from the valley bottom to the 4207-foot summit of Observation Peak, site of the old Trapper Lookout, and a panoramic view of the Wind River valley, or an easier ridge walk to meadows and vistas.

For the loop trip, drive Wind River Highway 15 miles north from Carson to Government Mineral Springs. Cross the Wind River and in 0.2 mile turn right on road No. 5401 for 0.4 mile to the trailhead, elevation 1300 feet.

Parallel a summer-home road 1 mile on Trapper Creek trail No. 192 and go right on Observation trail No. 132, steeply climbing the south side of Howe Ridge with fleeting views through trees. At 3 miles cross a small stream, which may be the last water. At 4½ miles the way swings around the north side of the ridge. At 6 miles turn right on Observation trail No. 132Λ and go a final ½ mile to the peak and views, views, and more views. For the return go back to the junction with No. 132, follow it west ½ mile, and descend Big Hollow trail No. 158 to Dry Creek trail No. 194, which ends at the same trailhead you started from.

For the upper start on Observation trail No. 132, drive Wind River Highway north 2 miles past the turnoff to Government Mineral Springs, turn left on Dry Creek road No. 64 for 6 miles, and go left 2 more miles on

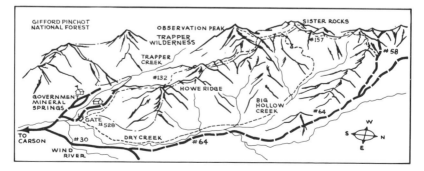

Trapper Peak and Mount Hood

road No. 58; find the trailhead on the east side of the road at the junction with road No. (5800)224, elevation 3200 feet.

Observation trail No. 132 sets out in virgin forest of Sister Rocks Research Natural Area, gaining 800 feet. At about 1 mile it enters an old burn grown up in huckleberries and flowers and drops 300 feet along the ridge connecting Sister Rocks to Observation (Trapper) Peak. At about 1½ miles the way enters Trapper Creek Wilderness, at 1¾ miles are trail No. 158 and Observation Camp (water is sometimes to be found in a spring on the north side of the ridge). At 2½ miles is the junction with the trail from Government Mineral Springs; a final ½ mile climbs the peak.

For an interesting sidetrip, wander meadows of flowers and huckleberries to the top of Sister Rocks, 4261 feet. Near the top are traces of an old trail, a few telephone poles, and bits of melted glass, all that remains of Sister Rocks Lookout.

SIOUXON CREEK

Round trip 6 miles
Hiking time 3 hours
High point 1300 feet
Elevation gain 400 feet in, 300 feet
  out
Hikable March through
  November
One day or backpack
Maps: USGS Lookout Mountain,
  Green Trails Lookout Mountain
  (No. 396)

Loop trip 13½ miles
Hiking time 8 hours
High point 4106 feet
Elevation gain 3000 feet in, 300
  feet out

The canopy is interwoven branches of tall firs, hemlocks, and maples. The floor is moss, oxalis, and ferns. The trail was reconstructed in 1990 to skirt the exciting waterfalls for which the valley is famed, and to stay in sight and sound of the ripples and tumbles of Siouxon Creek, a low-land stream whose limeade pools invite a person to mingle with the fish. Joyous camps are plentiful. Should a person feel energetic, the summit of 4108-foot Huffman Peak is handy for views of St. Helens and plenty more.

Siouxon Creek is an oasis between private and public tree farms, and it, too, was intended for the saw. The road was designed to go the length of the valley and the first 4 miles were completed and paved, but thanks to the concern of Forest Service employees, it was never finished. This may be the only remote trail with a paved road to the trailhead. The Forest Service has recommended the Siouxon River for a Wild and Scenic River classification, which could give the valley the preservation it deserves.

Drive to the headquarters of Mount St. Helens National Monument on

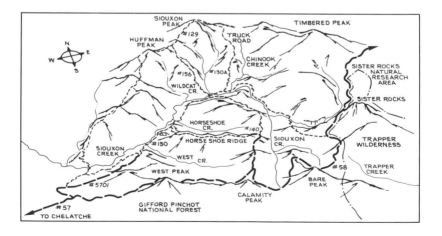

Siouxon Creek

SR 503 between the towns of Amboy and Cougar. A few feet north at Chelatche Prairie General Store go east on Healy Road. At 2.4 miles the county road becomes road No. 54. At 9 miles from headquarters, go left on road No. 57. In another 1.2 miles go left again on road No. 5701. At 11 miles from headquarters, the road switchbacks, intersecting the onetime beginning of the trail. Drive on to the road-end and new trailhead 14 miles from headquarters, elevation 1500 feet.

Siouxon Creek trail No. 130 plummets 300 feet to the banks of Siouxon Creek and a bridge across West Creek, then winds upstream on the valley floor past inviting campsites.

In 1 mile pass Horseshoe Ridge trail No. 140, which climbs to road No. (5700)320 and a 3495-foot promontory, former site of Horseshoe Ridge Lookout. At about 1¼ miles, the way climbs above a 60-foot waterfall on Horseshoe Creek, then traverses above a steep bank overlooking Siouxon Creek. In a scant 2 miles is the deep plunge-basin pool of a waterfall. At 3 miles is a crossing of Siouxon Creek on a bridge and a great turnaround point for a valley walk. Before returning, hike trail No. 156 up Wildcat Creek ½ mile to a waterfall tumbling into a rock cirque.

The promised scenic sidetrip and loop: Cross Siouxon Creek and go left on trail No. 156, a steep 1300-foot climb 2½ miles up Wildcat Ridge to Siouxon Ridge, then go west on Huffman trail No. 129 in trees, meadows, and rocky slopes to 4106-foot Huffman Peak, a former lookout site. The sidetrip is 3½ miles each way and gains 2700 feet, a lot.

For a loop: From Huffman Peak continue another 5 miles down the ridge to Siouxon Creek and 2 more miles back to the start.

There are other sidetrips and loop trails to explore in the Siouxon valley. Although some end up on logging roads, they all have something to reward a hiker.

63   DOG MOUNTAIN

Round trip 6 miles
Hiking time 5 hours
High point 2948 feet
Elevation gain 2848 feet

Hikable March to January
One day
Maps: USGS Hood River, Green
    Trails Hood River (No. 430)

The Columbia Gorge, where downcutting by the River of the West has kept pace with the uprising of the Cascade Range across its path, the river literally older than the mountains, is a national scenic treasure if ever there was one. Local private-property extremists still demand their "rights" and most politicians are eager to compromise the game away. A hiker can go far toward judging the relative merits of positions by walking a former stretch of the Cascade Crest Trail to a former lookout with views across the gorge to Mt. Hood and up and down the river.

Drive US 14 on the Washington side of the Columbia 9 miles east from Stevenson. Between mileposts 53 and 54 (MP 53.8) find a large parking area for Dog Mountain trail No. 147, elevation 186 feet.

In a long, steep ½ mile, the trail gains some 700 feet (watch for snakes and poison oak, both beautiful in their own ways but best enjoyed at a distance) to a junction; go right ½ mile to the first commanding view of the river. A lengthy zigzagging leads to the prairie–subalpine steppe, gaudy in spring with buttercups and asters, lupine and paintbrush, and scores of other blossoms. At 2½ miles, 2505 feet, is the site of Puppy Lookout, so-called because it was only partway up Dog Mountain. The cabin was on a shelf dug from the hillside. Here are the best river views; only the tip of Hood can be seen.

For more wildflowers as the season progresses, and bigger views of Hood, continue ½ mile to the top of Dog Mountain, 2948 feet, 3 miles. Do you have any remaining doubts about the worthiness of the Columbia Gorge to be preserved for the nation?

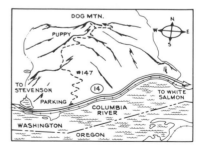

Dog Mountain trail

Columbia River from Dog Mountain trail

64 SILVER STAR MOUNTAIN

**Round trip from south side 11
   miles**
Hiking time 7 hours
High point 4390 feet
Elevation gain 2000 feet

Hikable May through October
One day
**Maps: USGS Larch Mtn., Bobs
   Mtn., Dole Mtn., Gumboot Mtn.**

The approach by road is a nightmare for the family car, but the path
through miles of flowers is a dream for hikers. The absence of forest and
the abundance of meadowland are the result of the largest fire in the recorded history of the state, the Yacolt Burn of 1902. The sky was so dark
in Seattle, 140 miles away, that street lights were turned on during the
day. When rains finally damped the blaze, thirty-five people had been
killed, hundreds of homes lost, and 238,000 acres blackened. The lower
elevations soon reforested and are now being logged. Centuries must
pass before forest advances foot by foot, year by year, to the heights. So it
goes in the way of Nature. Nigh onto a century later, hikers glory in

Silver Star Mountain trail

miles of ridge-top meadows carpeted with flowers, with only an occasional rotting stump to remind that there was once a forest here. The climax is Silver Star Mountain, site of a former lookout.

Five great trails lead to the summit. The route recommended here gives the most miles of meadows and a possible return loop.

Finding trailheads in the maze of county, Department of Natural Resources, and Forest Service roads is a challenge, and some of the roads are atrociously bad. A Forest Service map is essential.

From the town of Washougal on the Columbia River, drive the Washougal River Road, SR 140, some 10 miles. At a small country store where the road makes a right turn and crosses the river, go straight ahead for 0.5 mile, then left on Sky Road; follow it for 3.7 miles. At the county line, turn right on the Skamania Mine Road. A bit shy of 0.5 mile from the turn, go right, lose elevation, and cross a bridge; the road now narrows and starts climbing. At 2.8 miles from Sky Road go left on road No. 1200 another 4.3 miles to what the map calls Grouse Creek Vista, elevation 2375 feet; the trailhead sign only says Tarbell Trail (don't confuse with the Tarbell Camp on the west side of Silver Star).

On the north side of the road are two trails. On the left is Sturgeon Trail, a possible return loop; the recommended route, to the right, was part of the 1930s lookout road. Though ORVs have been barred for some time, signs prohibiting their use are missing and jeeps have climbed over the barricade, so the first steep mile is badly chewed up by machines, making walking difficult. At 1 mile the way moderates and enters meadowland covered with miles of beargrass, which blooms in mid-May. Looking back, see Mount Hood looming above the Columbia River. At 2 miles skirt Pyramid Rock. At 3¾ miles pass another CCC road turned jeep trail. At 4½ miles note the Sturgeon Trail (the possible loop route). A short bit farther go right up a steep, eroded roadbed to the 4390-foot high point on Silver Star and to views of Rainier, St. Helens, Adams, and more miles of meadows.

For variety on the return take the Sturgeon Trail. The distance is about the same, with the added attraction of a waterfall, but the big views and flower meadows are missing.

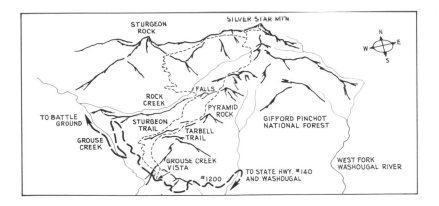

65 PACIFIC CREST TRAIL

The Pacific Crest National Scenic Trail, which extends from Mexico to Canada, is also known in the northernmost 250 miles by its older name, the Cascade Crest Trail. The 246-mile portion between the Columbia River and Snoqualmie Pass traverses highlands past three grand volcanoes and through the spectacular ruins of a fourth. The way isn't all pure fun because it also goes through lower, forested sections of the Cascade Range, where logging roads and clearcuts have savaged the wilderness solitude. However, the feeling of accomplishment gained by traveling the full length of the crest cannot be spoiled even by the worst of the messed-up parts.

Few hikers complete the route in a single effort; most do the trail in short bits over a period of years. Those taking the whole trip at once can start at either end; the south-to-north direction is described here.

At many places the trail is being relocated for the sake of easier grades or better scenery. The following brief summary is intended merely to provide a general impression of the route. For details of mileages and campsites, consult the Forest Service map and log of the Pacific Crest Trail, available from any Forest Service office.

COLUMBIA RIVER TO WHITE PASS

One-way trip about 148 miles
Allow 15 days minimum
High point 7620 feet
Elevation gain about 24,900 feet
Hikable in May the first 27 miles,
  mid-July for the rest

Backpack
Map: USFS Pacific Crest National
  Scenic Trail—Washington
  State Southern Portion

Begin beside the legendary "River of the West," skirt the slopes of giant Mt. Adams, enjoy views to what's left of graceful Mount St. Helens, and walk the airy crest of the Goat Rocks Wilderness—the most difficult, as well as one of the most dramatically beautiful, segments of the entire Crest Trail.

Drive US 14 east from Vancouver to the Bridge of the Gods and locate the trailhead parking lot on the north side of the highway, elevation 186 feet.

Hike through forest and lava flows with occasional views. The route is interrupted by logging roads, clearcuts, powerlines, and pipelines. Go up and down several times. Unless from the sky, there is no water the first 12 miles. The trail crosses Wind River and, shortly after, road No. 30. The way climbs to Big Mountain and then drops to road No. 60 and a dry camp. *Distance from the Columbia River to road No. 60 about 45 miles; elevation gain 7900 feet; hiking time 5 days.*

From road No. 60 climb miles of woods to Red Mountain and Blue Lake and the pond-dotted meadows and famous huckleberry fields of Indian Heaven (Hike 55). Pass near Bear Lake, go almost over the top of Saw-

Pacific Crest Trail near Snowgrass Flat, Mount Adams in distance

tooth Mountain, cross road No. 24, and continue through Huckleberry Meadows to Mosquito Creek. Cross road No. 8851 and traverse the east side of Steamboat Mountain to a crossing of road No. 88 to road No. 23. *Distance from road No. 60 to road No. 23 about 26 miles; elevation gain about 2900 feet; hiking time 3 days.*

The next stage is climaxed by the alpine gardens and glacial streams on the flanks of Mt. Adams. Cross road No. 23, traverse Swampy Meadows, and at 12 miles join the Mount Adams Highline Trail (Hike 40). At 22 miles leave the Highline Trail and at 23½ miles leave the Mount Adams Wilderness at Spring Creek and cross road No. 5683 to road No. 2329 at Midway Meadows. *Distance from road No. 24 to Midway Mead-*

ows about 29 miles; elevation gain about 3500 feet; hiking time 3 days.

Now starts the first long stretch of roadless country, most of it in the Goat Rocks Wilderness, including a couple of miles that can be dangerous. From Midway Meadows go a short bit along a rough road, round a lava flow, and at 6 miles enter the Wilderness. Proceed past Coleman Weed Patch, intersect the Walupt Lake Trail, and pass above Snowgrass Flat (Hike 34). Carefully, bewaring of hazards, climb the ridge above Packwood Glacier and traverse the shoulder of Old Snowy to Elk Pass (Hike 35). The route crosses above to McCall Basin, Tieton Pass, and Shoe Lake (Hike 28), at 34 miles leaving the Wilderness and descending to White Pass. *Distance from Midway Meadows to White Pass about 38 miles; elevation gain about 6100 feet; hiking time 4–5 days.*

WHITE PASS TO SNOQUALMIE PASS

One-way trip about 98 miles
Hiking time 13 days
High point 6500 feet
Elevation gain about 20,400 feet

Hikable mid-July through
  October
Map: USFS Pacific Crest National
  Scenic Trail—Washington
  State Southern Portion

North from White Pass extend miles of marvelous meadows and lakes and large views of Mt. Rainier in the William O. Douglas and Norse Peak Wildernesses, then a lower and more wooded (and road-marred) section of the crest leading to Snoqualmie Pass.

The first stage rarely leaves meadows and panoramas for long and passes numerous small lakes—too many to name here. From the White Pass Highway hike to Sand Lake (Hike 25), Cowlitz Pass, Fish Lake, and the Mount Rainier National Park boundary at 15½ miles. Weave in and out of the park, following the crest by Two Lakes and Dewey Lakes, and around the side of Naches Peak to Chinook Pass and SR 410; here leave the national park. *Distance from White Pass to Chinook Pass about 25 miles; elevation gain about 2400 feet; hiking time 3 days.*

The opening third of the next part lies in alpine terrain as before, and the remainder in woods broken by roads. Climb from Chinook Pass to Sourdough Gap (Hike 10), traverse to Bear Gap and around Pickhandle Point and Crown Point, with views to the Crystal Mountain Ski Area, ascend the crest, contour below the summit of Norse Peak, and drop into Big Crow Basin. Proceed to Little Crow Basin, a junction with the Arch Rock Trail, Arch Rock Camp, and Rod's Gap. Pass Government Meadows, cross the Naches Wagon Trail, and contour under Pyramid Peak to Windy Gap. *Distance from Chinook Pass to Windy Gap about 27 miles; elevation gain about 2500 feet; hiking time 3 days.*

Now comes a portion with few views except in clearcuts. From Windy Gap follow the crest nearly to the top of Blowout Mountain, descend in woods and clearcuts to Tacoma Pass and a logging road, and travel onward under Snowshoe Butte to Lizard Lake and road No. 54 at Stampede Pass. *Distance from Windy Gap to Stampede Pass about 27 miles; elevation gain about 1100 feet; hiking time 3 days.*

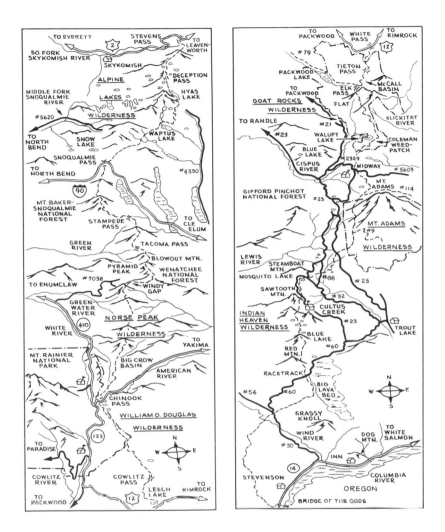

More forest travel—but much of the private land is being logged so the path is not always easy to find and not always pleasant, despite increasingly mountainous views northward. From Stampede Pass hike to Dandy Pass, Mirror Lake, contour Tinkham and Silver Peaks (Hike 3) to Ollallie Meadow and Lodge Lake, climb to Beaver Lake, and drop down ski slopes to Snoqualmie Pass. *Distance from Stampede Pass to Snoqualmie Pass about 18 miles; elevation gain about 1400 feet; hiking time 2 days.*

From Snoqualmie Pass the Pacific Crest Trail continues 253 miles to Allison Pass in Canada. See *100 Hikes in Washington's Alpine Lakes, 100 Hikes in Washington's North Cascades: Glacier Peak Region,* and *100 Hikes in Washington's North Cascades: Mount Baker Region.*

66   SUNDOWN PASS

Round trip about 15 miles
Hiking time 10 hours
High point 4103 feet
Elevation gain 2800 feet in, 300
   feet out
Hikable late July through
   October

One day or backpack
Maps: Custom Correct Enchanted
   Valley–Skokomish, Green
   Trails Mount Tebo (No. 199),
   Mount Steel (No. 167), Mount
   Christie (No. 166)

Good trail follows a loud river through big-tree forest, then poor trail ascends to heather meadows and a delightful lakelet. The lower valley invites day hikes. Riverbank camps tempt a person to lounge overnight, listening to the water, looking at the trees—and trying to understand why the South Fork Skokomish River was omitted from the Wonder Mountain Wilderness established in 1984.

Drive US 101 between Shelton and Hoodsport to 0.6 mile south of the Skokomish River bridge, turn upvalley on the Skokomish River Road 5.5 miles, and go right on road No. 23. Stick with it through many surprising twists and turns, taking care to dodge sideroads to Browns Creek Campground, Spider Lake, and Pine Lake. At 19 miles from the highway, go left on road No. 2361, pass a trailhead to Lower South Fork Skokomish River Trail, and at 24.5 miles come to the end of the road and the start of Upper South Fork Skokomish River trail No. 873, elevation 1300 feet.

The beginning is in deep forest interspersed with huge boulders that in the dim past were thousands of feet above, part of the mountain. At ½ mile cross Rule Creek and the South Fork on logs; by now, observing the beautiful large trees, you see why they were not given protection by the Washington Wilderness Act of 1984 (the Forest Service wants to make

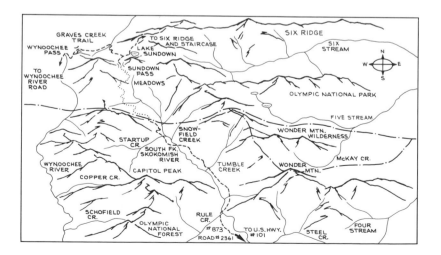

them into lumber) and why they are on our agenda for Wilderness Act II. At 2 miles recross the river on a log. At a very long 3 miles, a log spans Startup Creek to the last riverside camp. The trail starts up, for sure, and then contours steep slopes to the boundary of Olympic National Park, about 5 miles, 2800 feet. The good news is that here begins wilderness protection. What not everyone will consider even better news is that the wilderness is guarded not only by statute but by the end of good trail; the way trail beyond here receives little maintenance, is easy to lose, and shouldn't be attempted until all the snow melts, revealing boot-beaten tread, a help in route-finding.

Sometimes ascending ladderways of roots, other times traversing, the way is marked by metal tabs on trees and plastic ribbon. About ½ mile into the park is Camp Riley, in soggy meadows trampled by a herd of elk, many of whose trails are better than the official one. Cross the greenery and search for signs; if you go more than a few hundred feet with no definite sign of humanity, return to the last landmark and try again.

Beyond the meadows the trail climbs steeply, then levels out in a nice subalpine meadow. The trail appears to be intent on crossing the meadow but in fact only skirts it a bit before turning right, back into the woods; be wary, watch for tread. The trail tilts up and traverses to the right, ascending heather meadows dotted by small tarns. Above the highest, look for faint tread and ascend to Sundown Pass, 4103 feet, approximately 7 miles from the road.

Good tread descends 300 feet in ½ mile to a junction with Graves Creek Trail and in a level ½ mile reaches Lake Sundown, 8 miles.

Sundown Lake

MOUNT ELLINOR

Round trip to timberline 2½ miles
Hiking time 2 hours
High point 4500 feet
Elevation gain 1000 feet
Hikable July through October
One day
Maps: Custom Correct Mt.
  Skokomish–Lake Cushman,
  Green Trails Mt. Steel (No. 167),
  The Brothers (No. 168)

Round trip to summit 4½ miles
Hiking time 5 hours
High point 5944 feet
Elevation gain 2100 feet
Hikable mid-July through
  October
One day

From the top of Mt. Ellinor, Puget Sound and Hood Canal are laid out like a map, Rainier, Adams, and St. Helens on the horizon. In the other direction are Mt. Olympus, the twin ears of Mt. Stone, the double top of The Brothers, and the impressive cliffs of Mt. Washington. Look down into the Jefferson Creek valley to an inviting lake called Ellinor Pond, 2000 feet below.

From 1853 to 1857 George Davidson surveyed Puget Sound, working from the brig *R.H. Fauntleroy,* named for his superior, the head of the U.S. Coast Guard and Geodetic Survey. Needing names for the maps he was making, he drew upon the Fauntleroy family, calling the southern-most peak on the Olympic skyline Ellinor, for the youngest daughter, the double-summited peak for her Brothers, and the highest point for her older sister Constance. Later, Davidson and Ellinor were married. How-ever, subsequent mappers shifted Ellinor to a lower peak, replacing her with Mt. Washington.

One of the co-authors grew up nearby; back in about 1930, when he

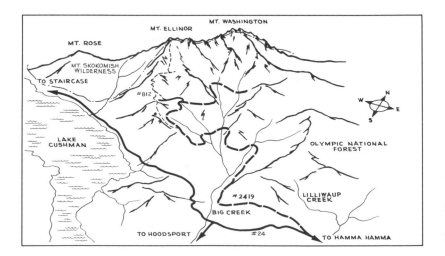

Mountain goat on top of Mount Ellinor

was 12 years old, Mt. Ellinor was the first real mountain he bagged. In those days the route began with a 5200-foot climb from Lake Cushman. Then, as now, the official trail ended at the first meadow. From there to the top was a wild and dangerous rock scramble. With more energy than skill, the climb was a snap. However, a logging road has shortened the trail to a mere 1½ miles, bringing the summit scramble within reach of folks with no experience and less sense. Slippery rocks, steep snowslopes, and rolling rocks loosened by climbers made many pay a high price. Recently, thanks to volunteers Frank Maranville (age 71), Frank Heuston (76), Tom Weilepp (61), help from the Olympia branch of The Mountaineers, and the Olympic National Forest, a new, safe (relatively) trail has been built to the top. It is still sketchy in places, steep all the way, but much less dangerous.

Drive US 101 along Hood Canal to the center of Hoodsport. Turn west 9 miles on the Lake Cushman Road to a junction. Turn right 1.6 miles on road No. 24, then left on Big Creek road No. 2419, past the lower trailhead at 4.8 miles from road No. 24, and at 6.4 miles go left on road No. (2419)014 to the road-end and trailhead, elevation about 3500 feet. Carry a full canteen; the slopes are dry.

Find the path climbing very steeply up the nose of the ridge. At ¼ mile reach a junction with the lower trail and keep climbing. At a long 1 mile, about the time the first heather appears, is the junction of Summit Trail. For the meadows stay on the lower trail ⅓ mile to timberline and trailend, elevation 4500 feet. The vistas of lowlands and Cascades are as good here as from the 5944-foot summit.

For the top, at the Summit Trail junction go left, climbing heather meadows, forest, rockslides, scree slopes, and flower gardens. The only consistent thing is the steepness, gaining another 1100 feet in a scant mile. In several rocky places the tread is faint. When the trail finally emerges on the summit rocks, watch carefully to note where the trail ends, lest on the way back you end up on cliffs.

The final 50 feet is a scramble, but the world opens up.

171

FLAPJACK LAKES

Round trip to lakes 16 miles
Hiking time 10 hours
High point 4000 feet
Elevation gain 3200 feet
Hikable mid-June through
October
One day or backpack

Maps: Custom Correct Mount
Skokomish–Lake Cushman,
Green Trails Mount Steel
(No. 167)
Park Service backcountry use
permit required

Two subalpine lakes set side by side like flapjacks in a frying pan. Above the waters and the forests rise sharp summits of the Sawtooth Range, a group of peaks noted among climbers for the odd texture of the rock, which largely consists of "pillow lava" erupted under the surface of an ancient sea and now eroded into weird shapes.

Drive US 101 along Hood Canal to Hoodsport. Turn west, pass Lake Cushman, go left on road No. 24, and follow the North Fork Skokomish River Road to Staircase Ranger Station and trailhead, elevation 800 feet.

The trail follows an abandoned road the first 3¾ miles, then ascends moderately but steadily in cool forest to a junction at 7¼ miles. From here a way trail goes left to Black and White Lakes in 1⅓ miles, Smith Lake in 2¼ miles.

The right fork switchbacks another ¾ mile to Flapjack Lakes, 4000 feet. One lake is quite shallow, while the other is deeper and ringed by rock buttresses; the two are separated by a narrow isthmus. The most striking Sawtooth summit from the lake is The Horn—known to a party of hikers who saw it on an autumn night years ago with the full moon (made of green cheese, then) touching its yearning snout, as "The Mouse."

Actually, the trip only just begins at the lakes. For high and wide meadows and broad views, walk the Mt. Gladys way trail 1½ more miles

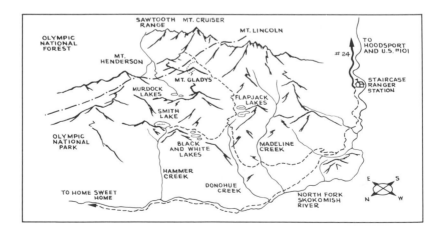

Upper Flapjack Lake and Mount Lincoln

up a lovely valley of rocks and flowers and bubbling water to Gladys Pass, 5000 feet, between a rounded garden peak and a vicious finger of lava. Roam the gardens to the 5600-foot summit of Mt. Gladys. Stare at the frightening walls of 6104-foot Mt. Cruiser ("Bruiser"), whose tower is visible from Seattle, standing like a boundary monument on the southeast corner of Olympic National Park.

Popularity has forced stringent restrictions on camping: between Memorial Day and Labor Day a nightly limit of 30 persons at the lakes and above; stoves-only at the lakes and above (wood fires permitted below Donahue Creek). Reservations can be obtained by calling Staircase Ranger Station (206) 877-5569. Alternative campsites are at Smith Lake and the scenic Black and White Lakes.

69   HOME SWEET HOME

Round trip to Camp Pleasant 13 miles
Hiking time 8 hours
High point 1600 feet
Elevation gain 800 feet out
Hikable May through November
One day or backpack
Maps: Custom Correct Mount Skokomish–Lake Cushman, Green Trails Mount Steel (No.167)
Park Service backcountry use permit required

Round trip to Home Sweet Home 27 miles
Allow 2 days
High point 4688 feet
Elevation gain 4000 feet in, 500 feet out
Hikable July through October
Backpack

In early May, when a small elk band is still in the Skokomish valley and trillium and calypso orchids are in bloom, walk the gentle trail to Nine Stream. In summer, climb from the valley to First Divide and broad

Mount Steel near Home Sweet Home, in late June

views, then drop to Duckabush River drainage and the lupine meadows of Home Sweet Home.

Drive US 101 to the center of Hoodsport (Hike 68) and turn west, pass Lake Cushman, and go left on road No. 24 to the Staircase Ranger Station, elevation 800 feet.

The North Fork Skokomish River Trail follows a revegetated abandoned road; thanks (no thanks) to the 1985 man-caused Beaver Burn, there are several views. At 4 miles the way turns into a real trail to Big Log Camp, 6 miles, a spacious area beside the stream. At 6½ miles the path crosses the river on a bridge over a deep, quiet pool. Immediately beyond is a junction; go right. The trail climbs slightly to Camp Pleasant, 7 miles, 1600 feet, on a large maple flat. This appropriately named spot makes a good overnight stop for springtime backpackers.

At 10 miles, 2091 feet, is Nine Stream and the end of level walking. In the next mile the trail ascends at a comfortable rate through a big meadow, then forest. After that the way is continuously steep and often rough. Flower gardens become more frequent. Mt. Hopper and Mt. Stone appear to the southeast.

At 12½ miles the trail reaches a meadow below Mt. Steel, turns sharply right, and climbs to the crest of 4688-foot First Divide, 13 miles, and views across the Duckabush valley to Mt. LaCrosse, White Mountain, and the greenery of LaCrosse Pass.

The path descends ½ mile to Home Sweet Home, 4198 feet, where one may enjoy the blossoms of avalanche lilies or lupine, depending on the season. The view of 6233-foot Mt. Steel is superb.

From First Divide a faint way trail goes around the south side of Mt. Hopper, but the route is rough and best left to very experienced travelers.

Many hikers continue 2 more miles from Home Sweet Home to the Duckabush River Trail with a loss of 2000 feet. From there they either proceed onward, climbing 2500 feet to Lake LaCrosse and over O'Neil Pass to the Enchanted Valley Trail, or hike 1½ miles downstream and then climb over 5566-foot LaCrosse Pass to Honeymoon Meadows on the Dosewallips (Hike 75). Only the vast meadows at the pass make this grueling 3000-foot ascent on a waterless south-facing slope worth the effort.

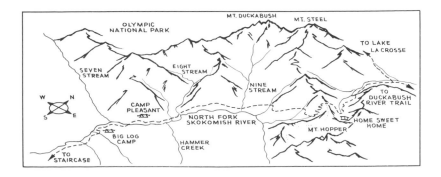

70   UPPER LENA LAKE

Round trip to upper lake 14 miles
Hiking time 12 hours
High point 4600 feet
Elevation gain 3900 feet
Hikable to lower lake April through November, to upper lake July through October

One day or backpack
Maps: Custom Correct The Brothers–Mount Anderson, Green Trails The Brothers (No. 168)
Park Service backcountry use permit required

Hike an easy trail, free of snow most of the year, through splendid forest to popular and often crowded Lower Lena Lake. The lake should have been part of The Brothers Wilderness but was left out because of a proposed hydroelectric project. This project would be so damaging to hikers that the Forest Service and environmental groups are protesting. But to add immediate insult to possible injury, the Forest Service has opened the trail to bicycles, thus effectively closing it to happy walking.

Drive US 101 along Hood Canal some 14 miles north of Hoodsport, cross the Hamma Hamma River bridge, and 0.5 miles beyond Waketickeh Creek turn left on the Hamma Hamma River road No. 25 and drive about 9 miles (about 0.5 miles beyond Phantom Creek) to the trailhead, elevation 685 feet.

The wide trail switchbacks gently and endlessly in forest shadows. At 1½ miles it crosses the dry streambed of Lena Creek, which runs underground most of the year. At 3 miles is Lower Lena Lake, 1800 feet. Here the trail splits.

The right fork drops to campsites by the lake and rounds the west shore ½ mile to more. For a great sidetrip, at a junction turn right to fol-

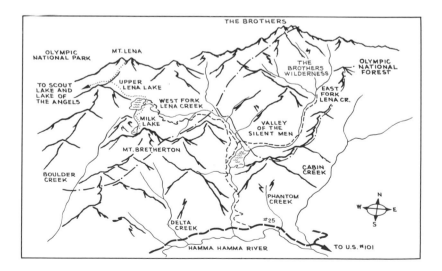

Upper Lena Lake and Mount Bretherton

low East Fork Lena Creek into the Valley of the Silent Men, crossing and recrossing the stream many times, toward The Brothers, a principal summit of the Olympic horizon seen from Seattle. This ancient miners' trail into The Brothers Wilderness is mainly used by fishermen and climbers but is well worth exploration by hikers who enjoy loitering beside cold water frothing and sparkling through rapids, swirling in green pools, all in the deep shade of old forest.

For Upper Lena Lake, stay left, following the West Fork Lena Creek, entering Olympic National Park at 4 miles. At approximately 5 miles, 2700 feet, the trail crosses a small creek, which can be hazardous during the spring runoff.

As the trail climbs, the vegetation changes to subalpine forest. Heather and huckleberry appear along with Alaska cedar. There are occasional views down the valley toward The Brothers. The steepness ends abruptly at Upper Lena Lake, 4600 feet, 7 miles. A rough up-and-down way trail rounds the north side.

Camps are inviting but have been overused, and some are being revegetated by the Park Service. Camp only at designated sites; stoves only, no wood fires. A privy is located near the inlet. The shore demands roaming, as do the meadows and screes ringing the cirque. For more ambitious explorations scramble to the summit of 5998-foot Mt. Lena, or ascend the creek falling from little Milk Lake, tucked in a quiet pocket and generally frozen until late summer, or follow a boot-beaten track over a 5000-foot ridge near Mt. Lena to Scout Lake, or follow the ridge by its numerous tarns toward Mt. Stone and Lake of the Angels.

Upper Mildred Lake and Sawtooth Range

HOOD CANAL
Mount Skokomish Wilderness

71   MILDRED LAKES

Round trip 10 miles
Hiking time 8 hours
High point 4100 feet
Elevation gain 2300 feet in, 600 feet out
Hikable mid-July through mid-October

Backpack
Maps: Custom Correct Mt. Skokomish–Lake Cushman, Green Trails Mt. Steel (No. 167)
No open fires

Three mountain lakes beneath the startling basalt spires of Sawtooth Ridge, well worth a visit—as they'd darn well better be, after the struggle. To keep the area primitive, the trail (way) is not maintained by the

Forest Service, and on certain wooded slopes is so obscure the hiker may not recognize it. What "trail" there is has been hammered into hillsides and over countless logs by the boots of generations of fishermen, hikers, and climbers. The distance is only 4½ miles to the first lake, but that doesn't include detours around wooden barricades. Nor does the figure given here for elevation gain include the ups and downs over logs and rocks and bumps. These are just extra dividends. But don't complain—even more than the official designation by Congress in 1984, they make it *real* wilderness.

Drive some 14 miles north of Hoodsport, and go left on the Hamma Hamma Recreation Area road No. 25 (Hike 70) to the end at a concrete bridge over the Hamma Hamma River, elevation 1900 feet. Find Mildred Lake trail No. 822 at the far side of the bridge and enter Mount Skokomish Wilderness.

In the first mile a little work has been done—logs cut, the tread occasionally graded. Such gestures end in the second mile as the way climbs steeply over a 3200-foot ridge and drops 300 feet to a delightful camp beside Huckleberry Creek, approximately 2 miles. The trail is easily lost here amid false paths made by elk and mixed-up hikers.

Cross the creek, stay level several hundred feet, then climb—and climb, with only an occasional respite, 1000 feet, mostly straight up on the stretch known as "Bailey's Boulevard." At 4100 feet is a ridge top of heather and alpine trees and great views that tempt a party to call it quits. Don't. The madding crowd has been left behind. The end is near. Drop 300 feet to Lower Mildred Lake at 4½ miles, follow the path along the shore to the lakehead, and near the inlet find the trail (again amid many false paths) climbing a bit in ⅓ mile to the upper lake and great views and great camps, 5 miles from the road.

The third lake, about the same elevation, is off toward Mount Cruiser. The path starts from the outlet of the upper lake. Despite the formidable approach, so many undaunted boots have tramped here that the lakeshores are being revegetated; be kind to the plants.

If time permits, ascend (with some bushwhacking) a 5000-foot knoll below Mt. Lincoln. The effort is repaid with a view of Mt. Washington, Mt. Pershing, and a score of other Olympic peaks.

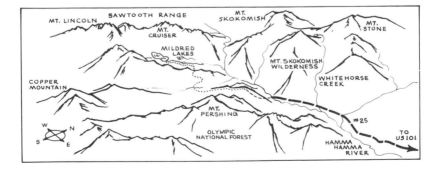

72 DUCKABUSH RIVER

Round trip 10 miles
Hiking time 6 hours
High point 1700 feet
Elevation gain 1300 feet in, 800
feet out
Hikable May through November
One day or backpack

Maps: Custom Correct The
Brothers–Mount Anderson,
Green Trails The Brothers
(No. 168)
Backcountry permit required for
camping in the park

The Duckabush River Trail is 20 miles long, wildland all the way to Lake LaCrosse and O'Neill Pass (Hike 96) in the heart of the Olympics, and the hiker who takes this respectful approach through valley forest truly earns the highland flowers. However, the lower stretch of trail, in 200- to 400-year-old firs and hemlocks, with sumptuous riverside camps, is a trip on its own, particularly enjoyed in late spring and early summer when the snow is still deep on the heights but is gone here, replaced by the blooms of bead lily and calypso orchid. It's not all a garden path; there are two major obstacles, Little Hump and Big Hump, but, for reasons to be explained, you shouldn't complain.

Drive US 101 some 22 miles north of Hoodsport to 0.2 mile past the Duckabush River bridge, and at milepost 310 turn west on the Duckabush River Road, which at 3.7 miles becomes road No. 2515. At 6 miles turn right on road No. (2515)011 and in 0.1 mile find Duckabush River trail No. 803, elevation 500 feet.

The trail gets directly to business, climbing the first obstacle on a long-abandoned road, gaining 400 feet in 1 mile to the top of Little Hump and the boundary of The Brothers Wilderness. Solitude is not assured from here on but Little Hump weeds out the pikers among the hikers.

The way drops 200 feet (oh! oh!) to river level and for 1 mile of flat valley bottom follows an old logging railroad grade through second-growth dating from the 1920s and 1930s. At 2¼ miles is a good camp.

Excellent if steep trail now tackles the main job—Big Hump. While toiling up 1000 feet, reflect that it was the Big Hump that stopped the

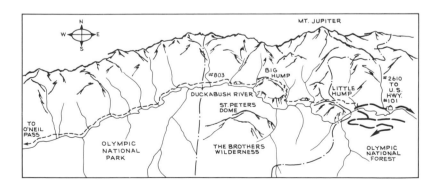

Duckabush River valley

logging railroad in the 1930s, as well as the truck loggers of later decades, saving this forest—which you will notice is virgin—for wilderness designation in 1984. So, no complaints. At 3½ miles a false summit gives views across the valley to St. Peters Dome and downstream, and at 4 miles the way tops Big Hump, 1700 feet. And promptly drops 600 feet (no complaints!) to the river and a great campsite at 1100 feet, about 5 miles from the road.

A scant 1½ miles lead to the park boundary and more camps.

73 MOUNT JUPITER

Round trip 14 miles
Hiking time 10 hours
High point 5701 feet
Elevation gain 3600 feet
Hikable June through October

One day
Maps: Custom Correct The
 Brothers–Mount Anderson,
 USGS Point Misery and The
 Brothers

Look from Seattle across Puget Sound to the Olympic horizon; right smack between The Brothers and Mt. Constance is Jupiter. Actually, the peak does not deserve rank in such distinguished company, but it stands so far out in the front of the range as to seem bigger than it really is. But give old Jupe his due: The peak offers unique combination views of lowlands and mountains. The summit ascent, however, is long and strenuous and usually dry and hot. Most hikers are content to climb to the views and leave the summit to peakbaggers. Carry a loaded canteen—there is no water on the way.

Drive US 101 along Hood Canal some 22.5 miles north of Hoodsport, a scant mile past the Duckabush River bridge. A bit south of the Black Point road, turn west 2.5 miles on unsigned Mt. Jupiter road No. (2610)011 to a junction. Turn left, stay on No. (2610)011, signed (sometimes) "Mt. Jupiter Trail," and drive 5 steep and tortuous miles to the trailhead, elevation 2150 feet. (*Note:* Due to a maze of logging spurs on state and private land, the correct road is hard to stick with and may at times be closed.)

The first mile switchbacks up south slopes of the ridge dividing the Duckabush and Dosewallips Rivers. At 1 mile, 2850 feet, the trail reaches the ridge crest and here leaves state land and enters Olympic National Forest. The hike to this point, with splendid panoramas, can be done in late May and early June, when the trip is really the most pleasant, especially since rhododendrons are then in bloom along the lower trail.

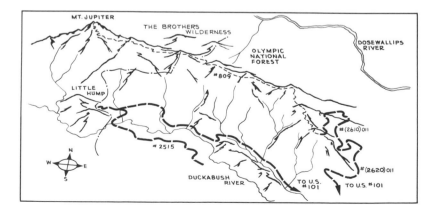

The Brothers from Mount Jupiter trail

However, the way goes on for those willing, following the ridge crest up and down, up and down, with more views. At 5 miles enter The Brothers Wilderness and finally climb a very steep final mile to the summit, 7 miles, 5701 feet.

From the summit, or from the trail, the views are glorious. North beyond the Dosewallips is Mt. Constance, and south beyond the Duckabush are The Brothers. Westward is the grandeur of Olympic National Park. Eastward across Hood Canal and the Kitsap Peninsula are Seattle, the Space Needle, suburbia, smog, civilization.

LAKE CONSTANCE

Round trip to the lake 4 miles
Hiking time 7 hours
High point 4750 feet
Elevation gain 3300 feet
Hikable mid-June through
October
One day or backpack

Maps: Custom Correct Buckhorn
Wilderness, Green Trails Tyler
Peak (No. 136), The Brothers
(No. 168)
Park Service backcountry use
permit required from
Dosewallips Ranger Station

A classic tarn, the deep blue waters ringed by alpine trees and heather gardens and sheer cliffs of Mt. Constance. But hikers must earn their passage to the secluded cirque the hard way, climbing 3300 feet in only 2 miles. The way trail is super-steep, dangerous in spots, and is not recommended for beginners or small children or the faint-hearted.

Drive US 101 along Hood Canal to the Dosewallips River Road just north of Brinnon. Turn west 14 miles to 0.5 mile inside the park boundary and several wide spots that serve for the trailhead parking area at Constance Creek, elevation 1450 feet.

The first mile is brutal, virtually without switchbacks, gaining some 2000 feet to a short, level stretch and a good forest camp at the 1-mile marker. The second mile seems even steeper, though this is purely an optical illusion caused by the ladderways of tree roots and the short rock cliffs. Feet must be placed with care and hands used for balance. Caution is especially essential on the descent. At 2 miles, 4750 feet, the trail flattens into the cirque. Camping restrictions forced by popularity include a nightly limit of 20 campers. (Make reservations by calling Staircase Ranger Station (206) 877-5569. Permits must be picked up at the Dosewallips Ranger Station, which has no phone.) Wood fires are banned; *please use the privies.*

Impressive as the lake is, the truly awesome scenery lies higher, beyond the portals of what old-time Boy Scouts, feeling spooky, used to call

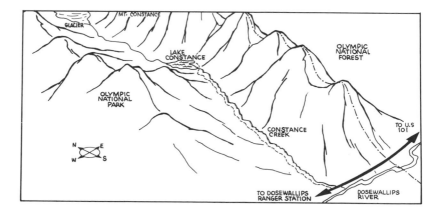

Lake Constance

"Dead Man's Gap." Follow a boot-beaten climbers' track above the lake, up talus, through the gap into Avalanche Canyon, a mile-long glacier trough between the east and west peaks of Constance. Solemn and spectacular it is, a place of crags, cliffs, and screes, snowfields and moraines. Hikers can walk safely to the canyon head at about 6000 feet.

The geology adds fascination. The weird, bumpy-looking walls of the canyon consist of "pillow lava" formed by molten rock erupting under the sea and cooling into these odd, rounded shapes. Heat and pressure metamorphosed limestone into pastel-colored rocks, often in variegated fault breccias of striking beauty. Hot mineralized solutions deposited green crystals of epidote intermixed with quartz and calcite.

75 ANDERSON GLACIER

Round trip to Anderson Glacier
  22 miles
Allow 3 days
High point 5000 feet
Elevation gain 3500 feet

Hikable mid-July through
  October
Maps: Green Trails Mount Steel
  (No. 167), The Brothers (No. 168)
Park Service backcountry use
  permit required

Follow a long trail to the edge of one of the largest glaciers in the eastern Olympics. Enjoy glorious views down the Dosewallips River to Mt. Constance, over Anderson Pass to Mt. LaCrosse and White Mountain, down into the Enchanted Valley at the head of the Quinault River, and, of course, across the Anderson Glacier to the summits of Mt. Anderson. In early August a wild array of flowers blooms, including small fields of lupine and paintbrush that stand out dramatically against the rugged background.

Drive US 101 along Hood Canal to just north of Brinnon and turn west on the Dosewallips River Road, coming to the end of pavement in 4.7 miles, Elkhorn Campground junction at 10.7 miles, Constance Creek at 13.5 miles, and at 15 miles the road-end and trailhead, elevation 1540 feet.

The trail starts in deep forest with a showing of rhododendrons in late June and, after going up and down a bit, reaches a junction at 1½ miles. Turn left to Dose Forks Camp and cross the river. At about 2½ miles the way again crosses the river, now the West Fork Dosewallips, this time on a bridge perched spectacularly some 100 feet above the water. The trail climbs steeply to dry forests high above the stream, which flows in so deep a gorge that often it cannot be heard.

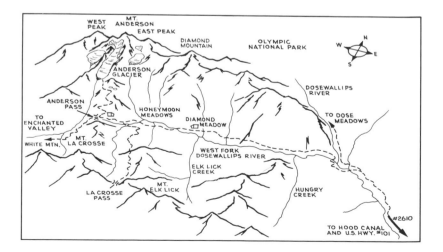

Mount Anderson from near Anderson Pass

The trail descends a bit to campsites at 5 miles, then climbs again, and with minor ups and downs reaches the small opening of Diamond Meadow at 6¾ miles, 2692 feet. Pleasant campsites by the stream. At 7¼ miles the trail once more crosses the river and begins a steady ascent, at about 8 miles climbing steeply beside the raging torrent as it tumbles through a narrow gorge. At 8¾ miles, 3627 feet, the valley opens into the broad, flat expanse and good camps of Honeymoon Meadows, named years ago by a Seattle couple who long since have celebrated their golden wedding anniversary. (Here and above, stove-only camping. And the valley is a happy hunting ground for a number of bears, so watch your groceries.) One final time the trail crosses the river, here a jump wide (a big jump), and ascends to Camp Siberia at 10 miles and Anderson Pass at 10½ miles, 4464 feet.

The Anderson Glacier Overlook way trail climbs steeply from the north side of the wooded pass, emerging from trees and in ¾ mile ending at a small tarn amid boulders and meadows. A few feet farther are the edge of moraine and the views, 5000 feet.

The West Fork Dosewallips Trail to Anderson Pass often is included in longer trips: a 27-mile one-way hike down Enchanted Valley (Hike 95); a 49-mile one-way hike to O'Neil Pass and out the Duckabush River (Hike 96); a 36½-mile one-way hike out the North Fork Skokomish River; and a 41-mile loop trip via O'Neil Pass and the upper Duckabush, returning to the Dosewallips with a grueling 3000-foot climb to LaCrosse Pass.

HAYDEN PASS

Round trip to Hayden Pass 31 miles
Allow 3–4 days
High point 5847 feet
Elevation gain 4250 feet
Hikable July through October

Maps: Custom Correct Gray Wolf–Dosewallips, Green Trails The Brothers (No. 168), Tyler Peak (No. 136), Mount Angeles (No. 137)
Park Service backcountry use permit required

Miles of marvelous forest, then alpine meadows waist-deep in flowers, where fragrance makes the head swim on warm days, where a quiet hiker may see deer, elk, marmots, or bear. All this and impressive views too, plus numerous fine campsites at short intervals along the trail. The pass makes a superb round-trip destination or can be included in an across-the-Olympics journey to the Elwha River, or in a 10-day giant loop over Low Divide returning via Anderson Pass.

Drive US 101 along Hood Canal to the Dosewallips River Road just north of Brinnon. Turn west 15.5 miles (the final 2 miles in the national

Avalanche lilies on Hayden Pass (John Spring photo)

park are steep and rough) to the road-end campground and trailhead, elevation 1540 feet.

A gentle 1½ miles through open forest in a dense groundcover of salal and rhododendron (the latter blooms in late June) lead to Dose Forks. A bit beyond is a junction with the trail to Anderson Pass (Hike 75); take the right fork and start climbing. At 2 miles note animal tracks at Soda Spring. Cross many little streams, nice spots for resting. At 2½ miles the Sunnybrook sidetrail heads up to supremely scenic but far-above Del Monte Ridge and Constance Pass.

As the path ascends, Diamond Mountain appears across the river; from a well-marked point, see Hatana Falls. At about 8 miles the valley widens and the trail crosses a series of meadows. At 9 miles pass the sidetrail to Gray Wolf Pass and continue in steadily more open terrain, with wider views, to Dose Meadow at 13 miles, 4450 feet; a sidetrail ascends to Lost Pass.

Beyond the meadows a bridge crosses a small canyon of a creek-size river with a lion-size roar. At 13½ miles, 4600 feet, the way enters the vast garden basin of the headwaters, surrounded by high peaks. The trail crosses the river one last time and switchbacks to Hayden Pass, 15½ miles, 5847 feet. In early summer a steep snowbank blocks the tread; be cautious.

Hayden Pass is the low point on the skinny ridge connecting Mt. Fromme and Sentinel Peak. North is Mt. Claywood, east are Wellesley Peak and the Dosewallips valley, south is glacier-covered Mt. Anderson, and west are the Bailey Range and distant Mt. Olympus.

Down from the pass 1 mile on the Elwha River side, just before the trail enters forest, find a delightful campsite by a bubbling creek.

For the across-the-Olympics hike, continue 9 miles and 4200 feet down from the pass to the Elwha River Trail and then 17 miles more to the Whiskey Bend road-end (Hike 84).

No wood fires are permitted above 4000 feet; carry a stove or a lot of baloney sandwiches.

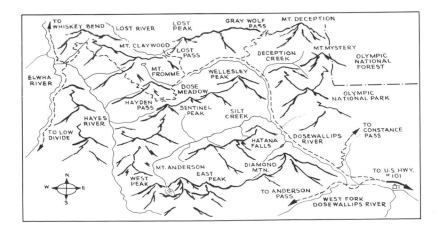

77 MARMOT PASS

Round trip to Marmot Pass 10½ miles
Hiking time 9 hours
High point 6000 feet
Elevation gain 3500 feet
Hikable July through mid-November

One day or backpack
Maps: Custom Correct Buckhorn Wilderness, Green Trails Tyler Peak (No. 136)

Before World War II, in an era when Boy Scouts were perhaps the principal wanderers of the Olympic wilderness, the "Three Rivers Hike" was among the most popular trips from old Camp Parsons. Thousands of Scouts now getting quite long in the tooth vividly recall their introduction to highlands on the grueling "Poop Out Drag," climbing steeply and endlessly upward along a sun-baked south slope, arriving in late afternoon at Camp Mystery, then taking an after-dinner walk through flower gardens and broad meadows to Marmot Pass and thrilling evening views down to shadowed forests of the Dungeness River, 3000 feet below, and beyond to Mt. Mystery, Mt. Deception, second-highest in the Olympics, and the jagged line of The Needles, all etched in a sunset-colored sky.

Drive US 101 along Hood Canal to 0.9 miles south of the Quilcene Ranger Station and turn west on Penny Creek Road. At 1.4 miles go left on a road signed "Big Quilcene River Road," which becomes road No. 27. At about 10 miles, go left on No. 2750, signed "Big Quilcene Trail"; in another 5 miles, find the start of Big Quilcene trail No. 833, elevation 2500 feet.

The trail immediately enters the Buckhorn Wilderness and follows the river through intensely green forest, all moss and ferns and lichen, crossing numerous step-across creeks, passing many close-up looks at the lovely river. At 2½ miles is Shelter Rock Camp, 3600 feet, and the last

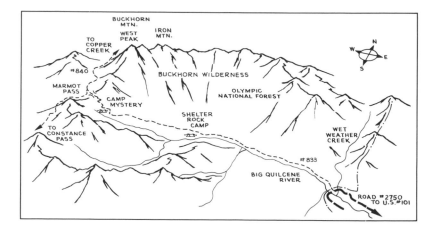

Warrior Peak and Mount Constance from Marmot Pass

water for 2 miles.

Now the way turns steeply upward from big trees to little, the hot, dry scree alternating with flowers, of the famous (or infamous) Poop Out Drag. At 4½ miles the suffering ends as the trail abruptly flattens out at Camp Mystery, 5400 feet, with two delightful springs and campsites in alpine trees. Except for snowmelt there is no water above, so this is the spot to camp.

The trail continues upward, passing under a cliff and opening into a wide, flat meadow, marmots whistling up a storm. At 5¼ miles, 6000 feet, the way attains the Buckhorn Botanical Area and, a bit farther, Marmot Pass and panoramas westward; as well as back down east to Hood Canal.

The Three Rivers Hike of saga and myth descended the trail 1½ miles to Boulder Shelter, followed Dungeness trail No. 833 to Home Lake and Constance Pass in Olympic National Park, climbed Del Monte Ridge, and plunged down the interminable short switchbacks of the Sunnybrook Trail to the Dosewallips River Trail, and thence to the road. The trip is still extremely popular, using a two-car shuttle.

Fine as the views are from Marmot Pass, nearby are even better ones. For a quick sample, scramble up the 6300-foot knoll directly south of the pass. For the full display, at the pass turn north on trail No. 840, leading to Copper Creek, follow it 1½ miles to just short of Buckhorn Pass, and find a path climbing to the 6950-foot west summit of Buckhorn Mountain. Especially striking are the dramatic crags of 7300-foot Warrior Peak and 7743-foot Mt. Constance and the views north to the Strait of Juan de Fuca and Vancouver Island.

MOUNT TOWNSEND

Round trip 11 miles
Hiking time 6 hours
High point 6280 feet
Elevation gain 3350 feet
Hikable June through November

One day or backpack
Maps: Custom Correct Buckhorn
  Wilderness, Green Trails Tyler
  Peak (No. 136)

Climb to a northern outpost of the highlands. Look down to the Strait of Juan de Fuca, Puget Sound, Hood Canal, and across the water to Mt. Baker, Glacier Peak, and faraway Mt. Rainier. In the other direction, of course, see the Olympic Mountains. The steep southeast slopes of the trail route melt free of snow in early June, and usually only a few easy patches are encountered then. Mid-June is best, though, when the entire forest road is lined with rhododendron blossoms, spring flowers are

Headwaters of Silver Creek from Mount Townsend

blooming in the lowlands, and summer flowers on the south-facing rock gardens high up.

Two popular trails lead to the summit of Mt. Townsend. The one from Townsend Creek, ascending the southeast side, is described here. The other, the Little Quilcene Trail from Last Water Camp, is perhaps cooler walking in midsummer but is not in as good shape.

Drive US 101 to 0.9 mile south of the Quilcene Ranger Station and go west on Penny Creek Road. At 1.5 miles from US 101 go left on the Big Quilcene River Road, which becomes forest road No. 27. At 13.4 (sign says "14") miles go left 0.7 mile on road No. 2760 to Mt. Townsend trailhead No. 839, elevation 2850 feet.

For the Last Water Trail, drive road No. 27 another 5 miles and turn left on road No. 28 for 2 miles, then left on road No. 2820 for 3 miles to the Little Quilcene River trailhead, elevation 4000 feet.

The Townsend Creek Trail ascends steadily in timber 1½ miles, and then opens out and steepens somewhat to Windy Camp, 3½ miles, 5300 feet. Pleasant camping around little Windy Lake.

The way continues upward in parkland with a scattering of small flower gardens. At just under 4 miles is a junction. The left fork climbs over a saddle, drops into Silver Creek, and climbs again to campsites at Silver Lakes, a sidetrip of 2½ miles each way; one small lake is on the trail and the other is hidden. The right fork heads up the mountain, topping the ridge at 4½ miles, 6000 feet, then following the crest, passing 100 feet below the first summit at 5 miles, and running to the most northerly part of the ridge and the second summit, connecting there with the Little Quilcene Trail and a trail down to Silver Creek.

Which summit is the higher? They are so evenly matched—the north 6212 feet, the south 6280, but seemingly lower—you must try both. Soak up the view over the waters to the Cascades and over the rolling meadow ridge of the Olympics. The rugged peaks to the south are Mt. Constance and its neighbors and, farther away, The Brothers.

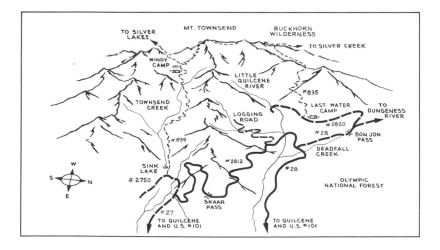

79 TUBAL CAIN MINE

Round trip to Buckhorn Lake 12
  miles
Hiking time 7 hours
High point 5300 feet
Elevation gain 2000 feet

Hikable late June through
  October
One day or backpack
Maps: Custom Correct Buckhorn
  Wilderness, Green Trails Tyler
  Peak (No. 136)

In the 1890s the Tubal Cain Mine promoters began selling stock like crazy and hiring mules to haul tons of machinery, steel pipe, 10-inch wooden pipe, and such truck as elaborate bedsteads to the prospecting operation, hauling out just enough high-grade ore samples to keep the stock sales going. Originally supplies were brought in over Marmot Pass, but in the 1920s the route shifted to the Dungeness River, on a 14-mile trail starting at packer Charley Fritz's farm. The digging (first claimed to be for copper, later for manganese) pooped along by fits and starts until the 1950s and likely isn't ended yet; old mines never die, they just are acquired by new stock salesmen. The frantically paced logging of the 1960s and 1970s has shortened the trail to a mere 3 miles. Hike the trail in late June or early July when rhododendrons are blooming the first 2 miles and the alpine meadows are flowered red, white, blue, and yellow.

Drive US 101 to 0.1 mile south of the entrance to Sequim Bay State Park and turn left on Louella Road. At 0.9 mile go left and follow the Palo Alto Road (which passes Charley Fritz's old farm), which eventually becomes road No. 28. At 7.4 miles from US 101 keep right onto road No. 2860. Pass East Crossing Campground, cross the Dungeness River, and start climbing. At 12.3 miles is a switchback and intersection with road No. 2870. Keep left on No. 2860. At 17.2 miles the road dips downward; at 18.8 miles recross the Dungeness River, pass through a gate (closed in winter), and at 22.7 miles reach the trailhead for Tubal Cain Mine trail No. 840, elevation 3300 feet.

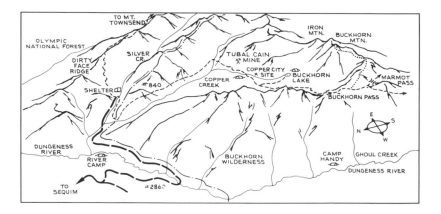

Tubal Cain Mine trail near Copper City

Cross Silver Creek and in ¼ mile enter Buckhorn Wilderness, passing under 10-foot high rhododendrons. At about 3 miles, just a bit above the trail, is a small mine shaft and a rough way trail that leads to the site of another Tubal Cain mining operation and a World War II plane wreckage in Tull Canyon, well worth the 3-mile round trip. At 3½ miles reach Copper Creek and the site of the Tubal Cain Mine operation, elevation 4350 feet. Marvel at the heavy iron pipe, 10-inch wooden pipes wrapped in steel wire, remains of old stoves, and a water heater, all carried in by pack train. The buildings collectively known as Tull (or Copper) City have rotted into the soil or been burned up in campfires (or some of them, on a memorable Fourth of July in the 1930s, blown sky-high by larking youngsters who found the absent miners' cache of dynamite). The main mine shaft is located a short distance above the townsite. (*Remember:* No mine tunnel can ever be considered safe.) The old building sites make an excellent basecamp for exploration of Tull Canyon.

The best is yet to come. Boulder-hop the creek to lush herbaceous meadows, the bright green gaudy-spotted with blossoms, and switchback a mile up steep slopes to about 5½ miles and a junction in a grove of trees.

The left fork goes in ½ mile of ups and downs to forest-ringed Buckhorn Lake, 5300 feet, 6 miles. Excellent camps near a stream a hundred feet above the lake.

The right fork is the entry to the sky, climbing meadows to the long, broad tundra ridge of Buckhorn Pass at 7 miles, 5700 feet, and views of valleys and mountains and salt water, then sidehilling rock gardens to Marmot Pass, 8¾ miles (Hike 77).

Royal Lake and Royal Creek valley

STRAIT OF JUAN DE FUCA
Olympic National Park

ROYAL BASIN

Round trip 14 miles
Allow 2 days minimum
High point 5100 feet
Elevation gain 2600 feet
Hikable mid-July through
    October

Backpack
Maps: Custom Correct Gray
    Wolf–Dosewallips, Green Trails
    Tyler Peak (No. 136)
Park Service backcountry
    camping permit required

Splendid forests and streams, an alpine lake and fields of flowers, surrounded by some of the highest and craggiest peaks in the Olympics. Allow plenty of time for the entry hike because the last several miles are rough and in places quite steep. Plan at least an extra day for roaming.

Drive US 101 to 0.1 mile south of the entrance to Sequim Bay State Park and turn left on Louella Road. At 0.9 mile go left and follow the

Palo Alto Road, which eventually becomes road No. 28. At 7.4 miles from US 101, keep right onto road No. 2860. Pass East Crossing Campground, cross the Dungeness River, and start climbing. At 12.3 miles is a switchback and intersection with road No. 2870. Keep left on No. 2860. At 17.2 miles the road dips to the upper Dungeness trail No. 833 at 18.8 miles, elevation 2500 feet.

The trail follows the water—always within sound and often in sight. At 1 mile, 2700 feet, is a junction of streams and trails; take the right fork, Royal (originally Roy) Creek. In ½ mile enter Olympic National Park. This far the way is entirely through forest, including beautiful specimens of fir, the floor sometimes a soft mattress of moss and other times a broad green carpet of vanilla leaf. At around 4 miles the trail begins traversing small flower meadows, each larger than the last. The path also steepens and becomes rougher. Ahead are glimpses of Gray Wolf Ridge and crags of The Needles.

The valley bends sharply southward and narrows. At about 6 miles, 4700 feet, the trail climbs a little cliff and enters the lower part of Royal Basin, an interfingering of groves of alpine trees, small meadows, and thickets of scrub willow. The trail crosses Royal Creek and several tributaries on flimsy poles; note the milkiness of the main creek, which carries glacier-milled rock flour. A final steep climb culminates at Royal Lake, 7 miles, 5100 feet. On the far shores are numerous campsites in the woods. Near the sound of a waterfall directly west is a large camp under the huge overhang of Shelter Rock; to find it, follow a path around the upper end of the lake and over a small knoll.

Several boot-beaten tracks lead to upper Royal Basin's high gardens. Any will do, but take care to skirt certain green, flat meadows, which in fact are marshes. Make a grand tour to the very top of the basin. Below huge piles of moraine, find a tiny milk-blue lake fed by the small glacier on the side of 7788-foot Mt. Deception. Continue to the ridge crest and look down to the fairyland of Deception Basin.

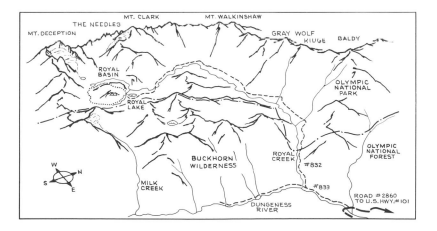

MOUNT ANGELES– KLAHHANE RIDGE

Round trip 7 miles
Hiking time 4 hours
High point 5900 feet
Elevation gain 1200 feet
Hikable mid-July through
  October

One day
Maps: Custom Correct Hurricane
  Ridge, Green Trails Mount
  Angeles (No. 135), Port Angeles
  (No. 103)

The simultaneous views of glacier ice and saltwaterways, the unusual geology underfoot (sedimentary strata tilted to the vertical), and the exuberance of flowers—these are reasons enough for Klahhane Ridge to be one of the most popular alpine hikes in the Olympics. Thanks to man's meddling, the scene also became famous (infamous) for mountain goats.

Drive US 101 to the east side of Port Angeles and go left 18 miles on the Olympic National Park Highway to Hurricane Ridge Visitor Center. Find the Lake Angeles–Klahhane Ridge Trail at the east end of Big Meadow parking lot, elevation 5225 feet.

Paved path leads east around a green hill to gravel path, which in ½ mile yields to ordinary mountain trail winding 2 miles along Sunrise Ridge, on the crest and around knolls. Just before starting across the south side of Mt. Angeles, pass a boot-beaten path leading toward the summit, the climbers' route. At 2½ miles sniff contemptuously as you pass Switchback Trail. (This shortcut climbs a steep ½ mile from the highway, saving the "bother" of hiking 2 of the best alpine miles of the trip. Aren't you proud you didn't cheat?) Continue on, zigzagging 900 feet up to Klahhane Ridge, 5900 feet, 3½ miles, and a junction with the Lake Angeles Trail. (By arranging transportation, you can descend this trail 1½ miles to Lake Angeles, 4196 feet, and proceed to the trailhead near

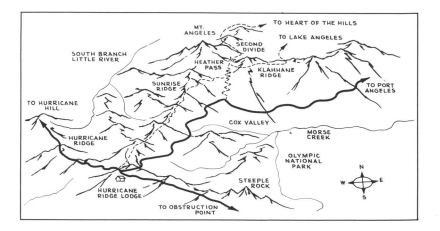

Mount Olympus and Mount Carrie from Klahhane Ridge

Heart of the Hills Campground, 10 miles from Hurricane Ridge Visitor Center—a superb one-way, downhill, meadow-to-forest walk.)

The views from Klahhane are as good as views get: the ice of Mt. Olympus in one direction, in the other the Strait of Juan de Fuca, San Juan Islands, Vancouver Island, and the ice of Mt. Baker.

Now, about those mountain goats. They were less native to the Olympics than bird-eating cats and rabbit-chasing dogs are to your house, for glaciological reasons never having made their way across the Puget Trough from the Cascades. In 1925 the state Department of Game introduced a dozen mountain goats to the northern portion of what in the next decade became a national park, no guns allowed. The bands grew slowly, and for years encounters were rare and exciting treats. Then, lacking predators, their population exploded throughout the Olympics, they became camp pests, and, worse than that, a threat to species of endemic plants that live no other place in the world, nor ever will if hooved to death here.

The Park Service has been compelled to take action. The cheapest and most humane remedy would be to hire professional marksmen to thin out the bands. This having been vigorously protested, the Park Service helicoptered animals out of the park and trucked them to other mountain ranges where, with no fear of humans, they are sitting ducks for the first guns they meet. Meanwhile, in the Olympics, years must pass before erosion scars are healed.

So much for blithely tampering with nature.

GRAND VALLEY

Round trip to Moose Lake 9 miles
Hiking time 6 hours
High point 6450 feet
Elevation gain 300 feet in, 1800 feet out
Hikable July through October

One day or backpack
Maps: Custom Correct Gray Wolf–Dosewallips, Green Trails Mount Angeles (No. 135)
Park Service backcountry use permit required

A Grand Valley it surely is, with three lakes and a half-dozen ponds in glacier-scooped bowls, but it would better be called "Kingdom of Marmots." There are meadows to roam and rushing streams and views to admire. However, the abundant wildlife is the outstanding feature: numerous deer and grouse and an unbelievable number of whistlers.

This is an upside-down trip—the trail starts high and descends to the valley; the hard hauling is on the return. Usually open in July, after a winter of heavy snow the road may not open until August; ask the rangers before setting out.

Drive US 101 to Port Angeles and turn south 17 miles on the Olympic National Park Highway to Hurricane Ridge. Just before the lodge turn left on a narrow and scenic dirt road through parklands along the ridge crest. In 8.5 miles, on the side of Obstruction Peak, is the road-end, elevation 6200 feet.

The drive is beautiful and so is the trail south along the meadow crest

Deer at Moose Lake

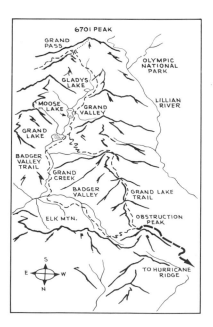

Camping in Grand Valley

of Lillian Ridge a mile, with views over Elwha River forests to Mt. Olympus, then swinging around rocky slopes of a small peak to a notch in the ridge, 6450 feet. Now the way drops steeply down slate scree and lush flowers to open forest on the floor of Grand Valley, and a junction at 3½ miles, 5000 feet.

The left fork leads in ¼ mile to Grand Lake, 4750 feet, then descends Grand Creek to 4000 feet, and climbs through Badger Valley to Obstruction Peak, reached in 5 miles from the junction. (The "badgers" actually are marmots; listen for their whistles.) This route makes an excellent loop-trip return to the road.

The right fork ascends ½ mile to Moose Lake, 5100 feet, and another ½ mile to little Gladys Lake. There are nice camps near Moose and Grand Lakes. (*Remember:* The minimum camping distance from lakes or streams is 100 feet.)

For more alpine wanderings, continue on the trail to 6300-foot Grand Pass, 6½ miles from Obstruction Point, then scramble up Peak 6701 to the west, with views to the Bailey Range and Mt. Olympus and Mt. Anderson and more.

If the weather turns bad when it's time to go home, keep in mind that the last mile along Lillian Ridge can be a battle for survival, even in July and August. In such a case it is wise to return via Badger Valley, several miles longer but mostly protected from the killing winds. Moreover, a wood fire is permitted at one site in Badger Valley.

83 GRAND RIDGE

One-way trip 7½ miles
Hiking time 5 hours
High point 6600 feet
Elevation gain 2250 feet, loss 1300 feet

Hikable mid-July through September
One day
Maps: Green Trails Mt. Angeles (No. 135), Custom Correct Hurricane Ridge

Never is the term "between heaven and earth" more appropriate than when walking the crest of Grand Ridge. On one hand lies the deep Grand Creek valley, the Olympic Mountains beyond; on the other is the deeper Cox valley, the Strait of Juan de Fuca, oceangoing ships, and mills of Port Angeles beyond. However, "heaven" demands a stern effort, the trail climbing up and down, up and down, high points of the ridge.

There is no water except drips from the lingering snowbanks of very early summer, so a party must either carry about a gallon a day apiece or make it a day hike. A round trip of 15 miles and 3500 feet elevation gain is a hard day in the hot sun, so a one-way trip is recommended. Ideally a friendly driver would leave you off at one end and pick you up at the

Grand Ridge trail on Maiden Peak

other; switching two cars around adds hours of driving. Logic says start at the high point, Obstruction Point, on the west end of the ridge and finish at the low point, Deer Park, on the east end. However, you will be tripping yourself up, looking behind to see the view, so the heck with logic. Start at Deer Park and look as you walk.

To reach Obstruction Point, the destination, from Port Angeles drive 17 miles to Hurricane Ridge. Find Obstruction Point Road at the east end of the parking lot and drive the steep, narrow road 7.5 miles to its end, elevation 6200 feet.

For Deer Park, drive US 101 to milepost 253, about 3 miles east of Port Angeles and about 11 miles from Sequim, and turn uphill on Deer Park Road. The first 5 miles are paved, then the way becomes progressively steeper and narrower. At 16 miles go right to the Deer Park Ranger Station and trailhead signed "Obstruction Point Trail," elevation 5250 feet.

The trail descends 1 mile to a 4800-foot saddle on an abandoned 1930s road (which in that age of exuberant car-touring was planned to go all the way to Observation Point!) The trees were cut as a fireline in 1988 during the Deer Park fire. From the low point the trail is mostly up and often very steep, traversing forests of Green Mountain. It levels off along a 5500-foot ridge top, and forest is left behind as the way ascends meadow and tundra to within 250 feet of the twin peaks of 6434-foot Maiden Peak, 4 miles.

The crags of Warrior and Constance and the glaciers on Anderson dominate views to the south. Deer Park and the salt water are to the west and Mt. Angeles to the north. Ahead are the naked slopes of Elk Mountain, daunting indeed on a day of blistering sun or roaring winds. The trail drops to Roaring Winds Camp (snowmelt only) and begins the 600-foot ascent of Elk Mountain. At 5¼ miles Mt. Olympus comes in view. At 5½ miles, near the 6600-foot high point of the trail, pass the Badger Mountain trail. In the next 2 miles along the broad, barren slopes of Elk Mountain, the glaciers of Mt. Olympus dominate the horizon. Across Badger Valley Grand Lake and Moose Lake and a tiny unnamed lake set in green meadows can be seen. Steep scree slopes lead down to the road-end at Obstruction Point, 7½ miles from Deer Park.

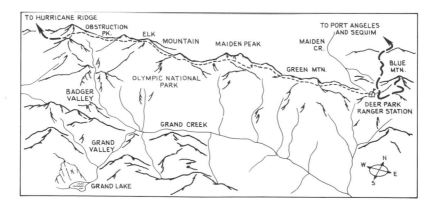

84 WHISKEY BEND TO LOW DIVIDE

**Round trip to Low Divide 57½
miles
Allow 1 week or more
High point 3602 feet
Elevation gain about 2500 feet,
plus many ups and downs
Hikable June through October**

**Maps: Custom Correct Elwha
Valley, Green Trails Mount
Angeles (No. 135), Mount Steel
(No. 167), Mount Christie
(No. 166)
Park Service backcountry use
permit required**

No whiskey, but a lot of waterfalls and forest scenery, can be found on
the 28-mile Elwha River Trail from Whiskey Bend to Low Divide. The
valley is very heavily traveled in summer, especially below Elkhorn, but
the natural beauty and historical interest more than compensate for
crowds. Spend a day or weekend on the lower trail—or spend a week hiking the complete trail, loitering at lovely spots, taking sidetrips. Before
setting out be sure to read Bob Wood's delightful book *Across the Olympic Mountains: The Press Expedition, 1889–90*.

Drive US 101 west from Port Angeles 8 miles and turn left on the
paved Elwha River Road 2 miles to the national park boundary. At 2.1
miles from the boundary, just past the Elwha Ranger Station, turn left
on Whiskey Bend Road and drive 5 miles (sometimes rough and steep) to
the road-end parking area, elevation 1150 feet.

The trail is wide and relatively level, the river occasionally glimpsed
far below, to Michael's (Cougar Mike's) Cabin at 1½ miles. Here a ½-
mile sidetrail descends to the old homestead of Humes Ranch, where elk
may sometimes be seen, mainly from late fall to spring.

At 4 miles, 1600 feet, is Lillian Camp beside the Lillian River. Pause
for refreshment because the next stretch is the toughest of the trip,
climbing 700 feet on the hot, dry Lillian Grade through an old burn, then
dropping for the first time to the Elwha River at about 8 miles, 1242 feet.

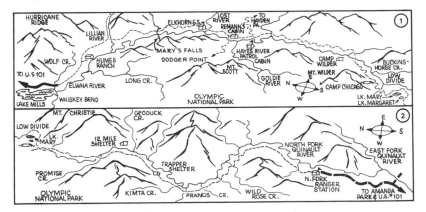

Humes Ranch

The trail goes up and down, never near the river very long, to a nice view of Mary's Falls, 8¾ miles. The way climbs again, passing a ¼-mile sidetrip to secluded Canyon Camp, and at 11½ miles, 1400 feet, reaches Elkhorn Guard Station.

The trail crosses an alder bottom where elk or deer may be seen and passes an old summer-home cabin of prepark days—Remann's Cabin, 13 miles, 1450 feet—and climbs again and drops again into Press Valley. At the upper end of the valley, 16¾ miles, 1685 feet, are Hayes River Camp and Hayes River Patrol Cabin, built in 1969 by 40 volunteer boys enrolled in the Student Conservation Program. Here is a junction with the Hayden Pass Trail (Hike 76).

At 21 miles, 1900 feet, is Camp Wilder. Easily cross a footlog over Buckinghorse Creek and at 26 miles reach Chicago Camp, 2099 feet, a jumping-off point for Mt. Olympus climbers. The trail now leaves the valley bottom and switchbacks in forest to the meadows of Low Divide, 28¾ miles, 3602 feet, and meets the North Fork Quinault River Trail.

To complete the classic Press Expedition cross-Olympics journey, continue from the pass 18 miles down the valley to the North Fork Quinault River road-end, for a total of 45 miles.

85 APPLETON PASS

Round trip to pass 14½ miles
Hiking time 9 hours
High point 5100 feet
Elevation gain 3300 feet
Hikable mid-July through
October (or until road is closed)

One day or backpack
Maps: Custom Correct Seven
Lakes Basin–Hoh, Green Trails
Mount Olympus (No. 134)
Park Service backcountry use
permit required

One of the most popular trails in Olympic National Park climbs to green meadows sprinkled with flowers, to views of High Divide and Mt. Carrie, and to possible extensions of the route to near and far places.

Drive US 101 west from Port Angeles about 9 miles and turn left on Upper Elwha River Road, paved all the way, 10.5 miles to the road-end, elevation 1840. Walk the abandoned road way 2 miles to Boulder Creek Campground (site of Olympic Hot Springs), 2060 feet.

From the upper end of the campground, the trail sets out in nice big trees growing from a groundcover of moss. The calypso orchids stage an annual riot hereabouts, usually in early June or so. At a junction in ½ mile, keep straight. The first mile is a breeze with only minor ups and downs. Then the trail crosses West Fork Boulder Creek and the work begins, the way climbing past two waterfalls to South Fork Boulder Creek. An unusual feature of the trail is the superb quality of the bridges and puncheon, which were built by meticulous craftspeople, including Penny Manning, a close relative of one of the co-authors. The path presents no problems but steepness until about 4000 feet, where mud grows deep and lush vegetation crowds in. At 6 miles are snowpatches that may last all summer (ice axes advised for early-summer hikers). At 7½ miles the trail reaches a 5100-foot high point and descends to 5000-foot Appleton Pass. The first 3 miles of the trail have several small established campsites.

Views at the pass being limited, take an unsigned way trail on the east

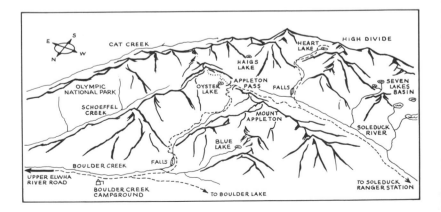

side of the pass and follow the ridge crest upward, through alpine forest past tiny Oyster Lake, into green meadows, and in 1½ miles to a 5500-foot viewpoint overlooking Cat Creek to glacier-draped Mt. Carrie. Camping (stoves only) is superb along the ridge when there is snowmelt.

From Appleton Pass the trail descends 2¼ miles to the Soleduck River Trail, reached at 6½ miles from Sol Duc Hot Springs.

Mount Olympus from near Oyster Lake

PYRAMID MOUNTAIN

Round trip 7 miles
Hiking time 4 hours
High point 3100 feet
Elevation gain 2400 feet
Hikable late May through
    October

One day
Maps: Custom Correct Lake
    Crescent–Happy Lake Ridge,
    Green Trails Lake Crescent
    (No. 101)

From Lake Crescent a delightful trail ascends magnificent forest to the 3100-foot site of a World War II airplane spotter's post. No enemy aircraft to watch for now except our own military jets, screaming over the ridges and scaring the breakfasts out of hikers, but there are views of a lake and mountains. A delightful trip, yes, but marred by a logging road to the very boundary of Olympic National Park. Ignore it, if you can.

Drive US 101 west from Port Angeles to the west end of Lake Crescent and turn right on the road signed "Fairholm Campground." Drive 3.2 miles to a spacious parking lot, elevation 700 feet. Walk the road back a couple of hundred yards to find the trail on the uphill side.

After a moderate start, gaining only 400 feet in the first mile, at 1½ miles the way steepens, crosses several small streams (perhaps dry by late summer), and goes through beautiful fir trees. The tread is mostly well graded and wide but on crossings of steep shale narrows to meager inches.

At 2½ miles the trail switchbacks to a saddle in the ridge marking the boundary between Olympic National Park and Olympic National Forest. A logging road here is a jolting reminder of the different objectives of park and forest. It also is shocking evidence of a contempt for wilderness—the road could just as well have been built farther below the ridge crest, out of sight, not disturbing the trail mood. Even though the forest probably will be clearcut to the park boundary, there was no need to put a permanent road that close. As it is, some hikers surely are going to feel so disheartened they'll drive the road and throw away the best part of the trip, making it a mere stroll.

From the saddle the trail stays on the national forest side of the ridge,

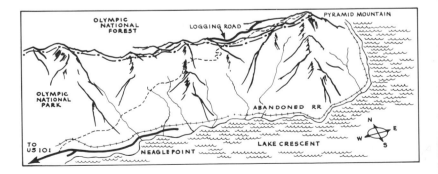

Lake Crescent and Storm King Mountain from Pyramid Mountain

generally a few feet from the crest. At 3½ miles, 3100 feet, it ends at an abandoned cabin perched atop a cliff dropping off on three sides. Here and in many other places in the Olympics during World War II, spotters lived the year around, watching for Japanese aircraft coming to attack Seattle and Bremerton. The view must have been better then; now greenery has encroached and one must peek around trees and shrubs to look down on the lake. On a sunny day the waters are dotted with boats. Directly across the valley is Storm King Mountain, but trees make it hard to see.

Mount Olympus and avalanche lilies on High Divide

STRAIT OF JUAN DE FUCA
Olympic National Park

 # HIGH DIVIDE

Round trip 19 miles
Allow 3 days
High point 5474 feet
Elevation gain 4000 feet
Hikable August through October

Maps: Custom Correct Seven
Lakes Basin–Hoh, Green Trails
Mount Tom (No. 133), Mount
Olympus (No. 134)
Park Service backcountry use
permit required (obtained only
at Soleduck Ranger Station)

Soleduck forests, tarns and gardens of Seven Lakes Basin, meadows of the High Divide, and views across the green gulf of the Hoh River to glaciers of Mt. Olympus and far west to the Pacific Ocean. The trail is so busy and the lakes so crowded that the biowelfare of the area has required limited camping in the fragile terrain, with more emphasis on day visits from camps in valley forests. By planning only to *look* at lakes and not camp by them—alternative sites are numerous—hikers can enjoy solitude even now, when the fame of the area draws thousands of visitors annually. A loop trip is recommended as a sampler of the riches, but the country is big and beautiful and offers a variety of wanderings short and long.

Drive US 101 west from Lake Crescent (Fairholm) 2 miles to the Soleduck River Road, signed "Sol Duc Hot Springs," and turn left. (At 12 miles stop at the Soleduck Ranger Station for a camping permit, if needed.) At 14.2 miles reach the road-end and trailhead, elevation

2000 feet.

The trail gently ascends splendid old forest 1 mile to the misty and mossy gorge of Soleduck Falls. Close by is a junction, 1950 feet, with the Deer Lake Trail—see the concluding segment of the clockwise loop described here.

The Soleduck River Trail continues up the valley of gorgeous trees, passes the Appleton Pass Trail (Hike 85) at 5 miles, 3000 feet, and soon thereafter crosses the river and climbs steeply to grasslands and silver forest of Soleduck Park and Heart Lake, 7½ miles, 4800 feet.

Shortly above, at 8½ miles, the way attains the 5100-foot crest of the High Divide, and a junction. The left fork runs the ridge 3 miles to a dead-end on the side of Cat Peak, offering close looks at the Bailey and Olympus Ranges.

Turn west on the right fork into a steady ridge-top succession of views far down to trees of the Hoh valley and across to ice of Mt. Olympus. At 10½ miles a sidetrail descends 1½ miles left to 4500-foot Hoh Lake, and from there to the Hoh River (Hike 89). Here, too, a path climbs a bit to the 5474-foot summit of Bogachiel Peak, a former lookout site, and the climax panoramas. Plan to spend a lot of time gazing the full round of the compass.

The route swings along the side of the peak, at 11¾ miles passing the sidetrail to Seven Lakes Basin (often snowbound on the north side until mid-August), and traverses Bogachiel Ridge above the greenery (and often, a band of elk) in Bogachiel Basin. Snowfields linger late on this stretch and may be troublesome or dangerous for inexperienced hikers who try the trip too early in the summer.

The trail contours the ridge above the Bogachiel River almost 2 miles, then in subalpine trees drops to Deer Lake at 3500 feet and a junction with the Bogachiel River Trail (Hike 88) at 15 miles. Past the lake the trail descends in lush forest to Soleduck Falls at 18 miles and another mile to the road.

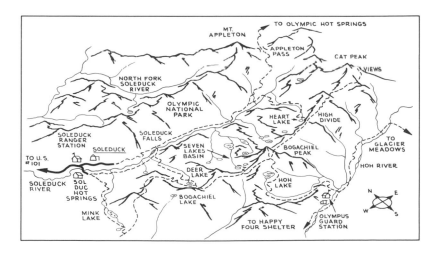

88   BOGACHIEL RIVER

Round trip to Bogachiel Shelter
11½ miles
Hiking time 6 hours
High point 560 feet
Elevation gain 260 feet
Hikable March through
November
One day or backpack
Maps: Custom Correct Bogachiel
Valley, Green Trails Spruce
Mountain (No. 132), Mount Tom
(No. 133)
Park Service backcountry use
permit required

One-way trip to High Divide 31
miles
Allow 3–4 days
High point 5474 feet
Elevation gain 4100 feet
Hikable July through October
Backpack

The Hoh Rain Forest or the Bogachiel Rain Forest—take your pick. They are alike as two peas in a pod, only the Hoh has a good trail and lots of people and the Bogachiel has a poorer trail and a degree of solitude, which is surprising for such a beautiful hike through large old trees, rainforest foliage, and luxuriant mosses. In autumn, the vine maple, alder, and bigleaf maple stage a glorious color show. Elk, deer, cougar, bear, and other animals may be seen by quiet and lucky hikers. A late-fall or winter visitor usually has the forest all to himself, the only footprints on the trail those of elk. The valley offers a superb day trip for virtually any time of the year, or a weekend for more extended enjoyment of wilderness greenery and streams, or a magnificent long approach to alpine climaxes of the High Divide.

Drive US 101 to 5 miles south of Forks, and directly opposite the entrance to Bogachiel State Park turn left on Undie Road, which passes numerous sideroads and eventually becomes road No. 2932. At 5.5 miles reach a gate and large trailhead parking lot, elevation 350 feet.

The trail descends ¼ mile and then intersects and follows an old logging railroad bed 1½ miles to the park boundary and 1½ miles more in

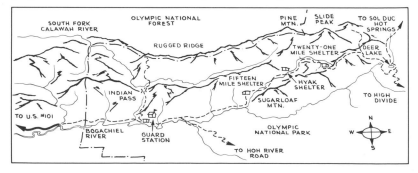

Bogachiel River (John Spring photo)

the park. Amid second-growth forest (logging done during World War II, on the excuse of "national emergency") look for giant stumps with springboard holes in both sides. Then virgin forest begins.

Bogachiel Shelter (emergency use only) and the old guard station, rebuilt by the Student Conservation Program, are 5¾ miles from the road and make a good lunch stop and turnaround point for day-hikers.

Near the shelter a branch trail climbs north over 1041-foot Indian Pass and drops to the Calawah River. At about 7¾ miles another sidetrail fords the river and climbs over the ridge south to Hoh River Road.

The valley path continues gently in lovely forest, never far from the river and sometimes beside it, to Flapjack Camp at 8¼ miles. At about 12 miles the river forks. While the trail follows the North Fork, the narrow but pristine main river valley can be explored on a sidetrip for 6 miles if you don't mind wading creeks and scrambling over high banks and fallen trees.

At 14¾ miles are Fifteenmile Shelter and a bridge crossing the stream. At 15½ miles is Hyak Shelter, where the valley narrows to a slot, and at 18¾ miles Twentyone Mile Shelter, 2214 feet. At around 21 miles the trail abandons gentility, steeply ascends a dry hillside above the North Fork headwaters to 4300-foot Little Divide 23 miles, then drops to Deer Lake at 26½ miles, and climbs in parklands to the meadow crest of the High Divide and Bogachiel Peak at 31 miles. For alternative trails to High Divide, see Hikes 87 and 89.

HOH RIVER– GLACIER MEADOWS

Round trip to Happy Four Camp
11½ miles
Hiking time 6 hours
High point 800 feet
Elevation gain 225 feet
Hikable March through
November
One day or backpack
Maps: Custom Correct Seven
Lakes Basin–Hoh, Green Trails
Mount Tom (No. 133), Mount
Olympus (No. 134)
Park Service backcountry use
permit required

Round trip to Glacier Meadows 37
miles
Allow 3 days
High point 4200 feet
Elevation gain 3700 feet
Hikable mid-July through
October
Backpack

From around the world travelers are drawn to the Hoh River by the fame of the Olympic rainforest. Most of the 100,000 annual visitors are richly satisfied by the self-guiding nature walks at the road-end, but more ambitious hikers can continue for miles on the nearly flat trail through huge trees draped with moss and then climb to alpine meadows and the edge of the Blue Glacier.

Drive US 101 to the Hoh River Road and turn east 19 miles to the Hoh Ranger Station and Campground, elevation 578 feet. The hike begins on the nature trail starting at the visitor center; before setting out, study the museum displays explaining the geology, climate, flora, and fauna.

The way lies amid superb, large specimens of Douglas fir, western hemlock, Sitka spruce, and western red cedar, groves of bigleaf maple swollen with moss, and shrubs and ferns. Gravel bars and cold rapids of the river are never far away, inviting sidetrips. Here and there are

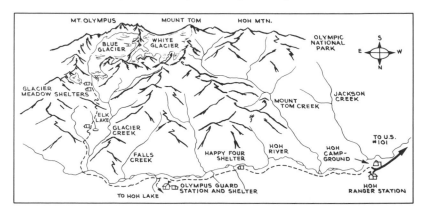

Blue Glacier on Mount Olympus

glimpses upward to snows of Mt. Tom and Mt. Carrie. In winter one may often see herds of Roosevelt elk; were it not for their constant grazing, the relatively open forest floor would be a dense jungle.

Any distance can make a full day, what with long, lingering pauses. Happy Four Camp, at 5¾ miles, elevation 800 feet, is a logical turn-around for a day hike and also a good campsite for backpackers.

The trail remains level to the next camp at Olympus Guard Station, 9 miles, 948 feet. At 9¾ miles is a junction with the trail to High Divide (Hike 87). The valley trail then climbs a bit to the bridge over the spectacular canyon of the Hoh at 13¼ miles, 1400 feet, leaves the Hoh valley, and climbs more to forest-surrounded Elk Lake, 15 miles, 2500 feet. (No camping within 200 feet of the lake; stove required.)

Now the grade becomes steep, ascending through steadily smaller trees, with views across Glacier Creek of snows and cliffs, to Glacier Meadows, 17¼ miles, 4200 feet (stove camping only). Wander a short way in flowers and parkland to a viewpoint near the foot of the Blue Glacier, where torrents pour down ice-polished slabs to the forest below. Or follow the trail ½ mile to the end of the bouldery crest of a lateral moraine. Admire crevasses and icefalls of the glacier, and the summit tower of 7965-foot Mt. Olympus.

90

THE OTHER
HOH RAIN FOREST

Round trip 7 miles
Hiking time 3 hours
High point 840 feet
Elevation gain 115 feet
Hikable most of year

One day or backpack
Maps: Custom Correct Mount
   Olympus Climbers map, Green
   Trails Mount Tom (No. 133)

The world-famous Hoh River Rain Forest has a twin named the South
Fork Hoh River. Maybe the moss isn't as thick on the trees and maybe
the trail is a bit rougher, but it does have something its famous twin
doesn't—a bit of solitude. In fact, compared with the other Hoh, the trail
can be described as lonesome.

Drive US 101 to 0.6 mile south of the Hoh River bridge and turn onto
the Department of Natural Resources Mainline Road signed "Hoh-Clear-
water State Forest." At 7 miles turn left on road No. H1000, signed "O.N.
(Olympic National) Park—S. Fork Hoh Trail 10.5 miles." The roads are
not well signed, so be careful at all junctions to stay on No. H1000.

In 7.5 miles (14.5 miles from US 101) keep left, following the sign to
"S.F. Hoh Campground." Cross the river on a cement bridge, pass the
campground, and switchback up a steep, short stretch. At 10.4 miles the
road forks right, straight, and left. Take the left, dropping to the trailhead at the curve of the road, 10.6 miles from the Mainline Road, elevation 725 feet.

The trail starts in second-growth spruce forest, at ½ mile entering
Olympic National Park. Ups and downs lead to "Big Flat," 1½ miles, a
large, open glade interspersed with vine maple, alder, and mammoth
spruce trees. From here the way goes from glade to glade, sometimes
close to the river (numerous campsites) and other times out of sight and
sound of the water. At 2½ miles is Camp Stick-in-the-Eye. At approximately 3½ miles, 840 feet, trail maintenance ceases but the trail continues on another mile, often obscured in tall grass.

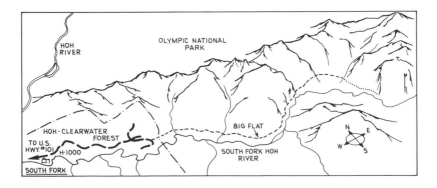

In the summer the river runs milky, fed as it is by glaciers on the southeast side of Mt. Olympus. The peaks at the head of the valley rise above timberline but are not named on the USGS map.

South Fork Hoh River

Fording the Queets River in mid-August

PACIFIC OCEAN
Olympic National Park

 THE QUEETS

Round trip to Spruce Bottom 10 miles
Hiking time 5 hours

Round trip to Bob Creek 22 miles
Allow 2 days

Round trip to Pelton Creek 32 miles
Allow 3 days

High point 800 feet
Elevation gain 600 feet
Hikable August through September
Maps: Custom Correct Queets, Green Trails Kloochman Rock (No. 165)
Park Service backcountry use permits required for camping

The best rain forest (yes, the best!) in the Olympics, old homesteads, elk, and more solitude than in other valleys of Olympic National Park. The first 5 miles have a few mudholes but overall are as good as any trail in the park. Why the solitude? Because the Queets River must be forded, not easy any time of the year and dangerous except in the low water of late summer.

Drive US 101 some 17 miles west of Lake Quinault and go right 13½ miles to the end of the Queets River Road, the trailhead, and the ford, elevation 275 feet.

Prepare carefully for the ford. Stout shoes—preferably boots—must be worn to secure placement among the large, slippery boulders. (The neatest trick is to take off boots and socks, don boots only, cross, and on the far side, empty water from the boots and don dry socks, then boots.) A stout pole must be carried to act as a third leg in the swift current. Scout around for a stretch of river that is wide and thus shallower and slower than the narrows; this may vary from year to year.

Once across, walk into the forest a short distance and find the trail, which utilizes a primitive road that was abandoned at least 50 years ago. Go upstream, winding through moss-festooned trees on almost lawnlike ground mowed by elk. In 1½ miles is Andrews' Ranch, a large field, and the remains of a barn built in the 1920s and abandoned in the 1940s. Look up at Kloochman Rock, an old lookout site on the park boundary.

In a scant 2 miles, don't miss the ¼-mile sidetrail up Coal Creek to the world's largest recorded Douglas fir tree, 17 feet in diameter. The top is missing, but even so the tree is still an impressive 221 feet tall.

For the next 2 miles, the way passes spectacular moss-covered trees to a junction of the lower Tshletshy Trail. In another ¾ mile pass Spruce Bottom and a series of campsites, beyond which the trail deteriorates, detouring around fallen giants and slides.

At 5½ miles is the Upper Tshletshy junction. Walk the abandoned trail to the river for a view across the water to Smith's Hunting Lodge, abandoned.

The trail gets progressively worse, though generally easy to follow. At 11½ miles cross Bob Creek to campsites. If time permits, follow Bob Creek upstream to a series of waterfalls.

The trail ends at 800 feet, 16 miles from the road-end, at Pelton Creek shelter, one of the few that have not been destroyed by nature or park rangers.

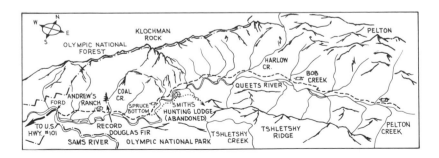

92 SKYLINE TRAIL–NORTH FORK QUINAULT LOOP

Loop trip 47 miles
Allow 4 days minimum
High point 5200 feet
Elevation gain 8550 feet overall
Hikable August through
September

Maps: Custom Correct
Quinault–Colonel Bob; USGS
Bunch Lake, Kimta Peak, and
Mount Christie
Park Service backcountry use
permit required

Ascend from moss-covered giants of the rainforest to sky-open meadows, high alpine lakes, and, finally, to ridge-top tundras. See for yourself the diversity of the national park that extends from the Pacific Ocean to glaciers of Mt. Olympus. However, this supreme journey is not for everyone. Only the most experienced routefinders and energetic hikers should tackle the Skyline Trail, which is intended to give a wilderness experience and thus receives only minimal maintenance. Hikers must expect fallen trees, wet brush, and soggy bogs. Even when visible the trail can be discouraging. On ridges it disappears altogether, becoming a rough route up cliffs and over gorges, the way only marked by occasional cairns, which dissolve to nothing when clouds envelop the highlands; miserable hours may be spent probing this way and that for safe passage. Every difficulty, such as a band of rocks, a creek crossing, a traverse, or a climb is succeeded by a long descent, which, of course, leads to another long ascent.

Drive US 101 north from Aberdeen and go off on the South-Shore Lake Quinault Road 13 miles to an intersection. Turn left, cross the Quinault River, and take an immediate right on the North Fork Road 3.5 miles to the road-end, elevation 450 feet.

The first 16 miles to Low Divide lie along the North Fork Quinault River Trail through glades of giant trees hung with moss, climbing gradually to the 3602-foot pass. The trail is wide and the woods deep. Campsites are numerous.

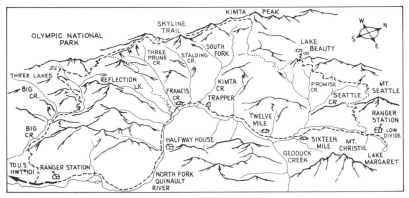

Camping at Lake Beauty

The Skyline Trail begins in an open meadow on the south side of Low Divide, heading back down the valley ½ mile, then beginning the first climb, over a shoulder of Mt. Seattle. The path is rough and narrow but easy to follow in the forest. In the meadows it becomes vanishingly faint, demanding detective work. In early August, when snow still lingers in creek beds, caution must be taken at crossings where snow bridges may be collapsible.

The tread is moderately decent the first 7.7 miles from Low Divide to the scenic campsite at Lake Beauty, 4670 feet. From Lake Beauty to Kimta Peak the difficulties are worse. The traverse that looks so easy on the map is broken by descents to get around rock walls and across creeks, steep climbs up rocky hillsides. Don't miss a cairn! Beyond the crossing from Promise Creek to Kimta Creek drainage, at the edge of an old burn, the trail is still rough and difficult but much easier to follow.

Skirt around Kimta Peak at 5200 feet and feast on the final great view of the ocean, the Queets River, and the entire Olympic range. Descend to Three Prune Meadows, 3650 feet, the trail now wide and well graded. At 20¾ miles from Low Divide, pass a sidetrail down to the North Fork Quinault Trail, climb over a 4000-foot ridge, and descend 3 miles past several small ponds to Three Lakes, 3200 feet. The next 6½ miles are an easy descent on well-graded trail to the North Fork Road. Walk the road upvalley ¾ mile to complete the loop.

93 COLONEL BOB MOUNTAIN

Round trip, north side, 14½ miles
Allow 2 days
High point 4492 feet
Elevation gain 4220 feet
Hikable July through mid-
October
Maps: Custom Correct
Quinault–Colonel Bob, Green
Trails Quinault Lake (No. 197),
Grisdale (No. 198)

Round trip, south side, 8½ miles
Hiking time 7 hours
Elevation gain 3500 feet
One day or backpack

Climb to a western outpost of the Olympic Mountains, a former lookout site with views of Olympics nearby and, farther off, volcanoes of the Cascades—St. Helens, Adams, and Rainier. There's water to see, too—look down on sparkling Quinault Lake and out to the Pacific Ocean, particularly spectacular with the sun dunking into it of an evening.

There are two ways, both very steep, to Colonel Bob: The south approach gains 3500 feet; the north climbs 4220 feet and is 3 miles longer.

For the north side drive US 101 to near its crossing of the Quinault River and turn east on the South Shore Road. In 2.5 miles pass the Quinault Ranger Station and at 6 miles spot a sign, "Colonel Bob Trail" (No. 851). Turn onto a narrow road, which promptly opens to a large parking lot, elevation 270 feet.

The trail climbs through beautiful rainforest in long, sweeping switchbacks, then sidehills, still going steadily up. At 3 miles is a crossing of Ewell's Creek and at 4 miles campsites at Mulkey Shelter, 2550 feet. Now the way switchbacks steeply to a 3250-foot pass and drops a bit, at 5½ miles reaching a junction, 2900 feet, with the trail from the south.

For the south-side approach to this junction, drive US 101 north 25½ miles from Hoquiam and turn east on road No. 22, signed "Donkey Creek Road, Humptulips Guard Station." At 8.2 miles, where pavement ends, turn left on road No. 2204, signed "Campbell Tree Grove Campground," and proceed 11 miles to a sign, "Petes Creek Trail" (No. 858), near the crossing of Petes Creek, elevation 1000 feet.

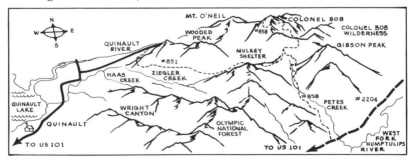

Near summit of Colonel Bob Mountain

The trail starts on the uphill side of the road and is steadily steep and in places rocky. At 1 mile is a crossing of Petes Creek, underground here most of the year. At 2 miles is a small camp, beyond which is Gibson Slide and then, at 2½ miles, the junction.

About 1 mile beyond, at 6½ miles from the north trailhead and 3⅓ from the south, is Moonshine Flats, featuring all-year water, the most popular camp on the route. At 1¾ miles from the junction, the way emerging from forest into flowers, is the summit, the last few feet to the top blasted from rock.

Few traces of the old lookout cabin remain on the 4492-foot summit. But the views are as glorious as ever. For sunset watching, camps can be found ¼ mile back, 200 feet below the trail, on a wide, rocky bench covered with snow much of the summer. Bring a stove for cooking; melt snow for water.

94   PONY BRIDGE

Round trip 5 miles
Hiking time 3 hours
High point 1178 feet
Elevation gain 550 feet in, 275 feet
    out

Hikable most of the year
One day
Maps: Custom Correct Enchanted
    Valley–Skokomish, Green
    Trails Mount Christie (No. 166)

Hike through a forest of tall, straight trees 4, 5, and 6 feet in diameter to where the Quinault River flows through a lovely canyon walled with masses of maidenhair ferns. Do this trip in winter and spring when the river is raging, or on a hot day in late summer when dipping in a deep pool can be inviting. A day hike is recommended, but there are campsites; for these a Park Service backcountry permit is required.

Drive US 101 to the South Shore Lake Quinault Road. Turn easterly, skirting the lake and winding up the valley. Pavement ends at 12 miles. In 13 miles pass the bridge to the North Fork and at 18 miles Graves Creek Campground. Continue on the final narrow road to the trailhead 18.5 miles from US 101, elevation 646 feet.

The trail immediately crosses Graves Creek on a high log bridge and climbs an abandoned road, passing beneath towering trees that are guaranteed to give a stiff neck looking up, up, up. The cut sections of giants that have fallen across the trail give a graphic measure of their size and age.

In a scant 2 miles the way reaches the high point and the end of roadbed. True trail now descends to Pony Bridge across the canyon of the Quinault River, 2½ miles from Graves Creek, 906 feet.

The bridge is a spectacular viewing platform any time, awesome during the roaring snowmelt season. When winter and spring floods are over, on the far side of the bridge two steep scramble trails lead down to the water's edge and tiny beaches. However, the best dunking spot is on the near side of the bridge. Walk back on the trail 100–200 feet and find a scramble trail going downstream to the rocks sculptured by water and

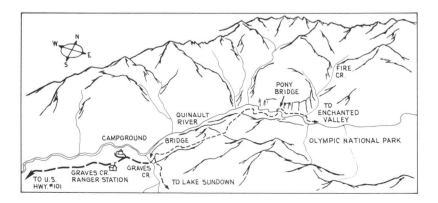

Pony Bridge

partially covered by moss. Most of the pools have a current running through; a deep pool in a back eddy makes an ideal swimming hole.

Be careful of the canyon rim—parts are even overhung. This is *not* a place to let small children gambol.

Carpet of oxalis along the Quinault Valley Trail

PACIFIC OCEAN
Olympic National Park

95   ENCHANTED VALLEY

Round trip 26 miles
Allow 2–3 days
High point 1957 feet
Elevation gain 1300 feet, plus ups
    and downs
Hikable March through
    December

Maps: Custom Correct Enchanted
    Valley–Skokomish, Green
    Trails Mount Christie (No. 166),
    Mount Steel (No. 167)
Park Service backcountry use
    permit required

Walk beside the river in open alder and maple forest, and miles through cathedral-like fir forest where future generations of loggers will come to see what their grandfathers meant when they boasted of big trees. The climax is Enchanted Valley, a large alpine cirque ringed by 3000-foot cliffs. The trail has many minor ups and downs and during rainy spells is a muddy mess, but in such country, who can complain?

Drive to the Quinault River trailhead and follow the trail 2½ miles to Pony Bridge, as described in Hike 94.

Cross Pony Bridge over the Quinault River, admiring the lovely canyon. In another ½ mile climb around the canyon and drop back to the river. For the next 10 miles the way alternates, up and down, between flat bottoms (alders and maples) and terraces several hundred feet above the river (groves of tall fir and cedar). With any luck a hiker should see elk. At 6½ miles pass a junction to O'Neil Creek Camp, ¼ mile off the main track.

All along are tantalizing glimpses of peaks above, but at about 10½ miles the change from lowlands to alpine is dramatic. Suddenly one leaves deep forest and bursts into the mountain world of rock and ice. To the left are cliffs of 6911-foot Chimney Peak. To the right is 6400-foot White Mountain. Both are dominated by the twin peaks of Mt. Anderson, divided by a small glacier: The sharp pyramid is 7366-foot West Peak, the highest point; the more massive peak in the middle is 7321 feet.

Coming down to earth, the valley has widened out. The lower part is floored with dense brush but farther up are flower fields. At 13 miles cross the Quinault River, now a small creek. Walk a short bit through meadows to the three-story Enchanted Valley Chalet, built in 1930 as a commercial hotel and now maintained by the Park Service as a public shelter. The structure often is full (only part of the lower floor is open to camping) so be prepared to camp out. Be sure to carry a stove; cooking facilities are limited in the chalet and wood may be wet outside. Those unable to do the full 13 miles in a single day can stop overnight at any of a number of camps along the way.

Beyond the chalet the trail climbs 2500 feet in 4½ miles to 4500-foot Anderson Pass, at 2 miles passing the largest known living western hemlock, 8 feet, 8 inches in diameter. It then descends the West Fork Dosewallips River 10 miles to the road (Hike 75). Another trail leads to O'Neil Pass, Hart and Marmot Lakes, and Lake LaCrosse (Hike 96).

What's the best season for the trip? Well, some winters there is little snow in the lower valley, which thus can be walked in December or March when hardly any other country is open. Early spring is wonderful, when birds are singing, shrubs and maples are exploding with new leaves, yellow violet and oxalis are blooming, and waterfalls and avalanches tumble and slide down cliffs. So is summer, when alders and maples canopy the valley bottoms in cool green. But fall is also glorious, with bigleaf maples yellowing and the trail lost in fallen leaves. Better try it in all seasons.

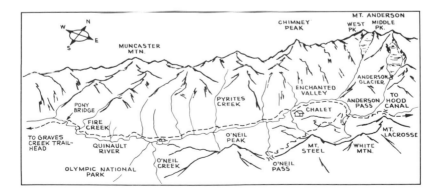

96 LAKE LaCROSSE–O'NEIL PASS

One-way trip to Lake LaCrosse
via Quinault River and
O'Neil Pass 26¾ miles
Allow 5 days minimum, by any
route
High point 4900 feet
Elevation gain 4000 feet
Hikable mid-July through
September

Maps: Custom Correct Enchanted
Valley–Skokomish, Green
Trails Mount Steel (No. 167),
Mount Christie (No. 166)
Park Service backcountry use
permit required

In the heart of the Olympic wilderness, 25 miles from the nearest road, a group of beautiful alpine lakes sparkle amid a wonderland of heather and huckleberries. Quicker ways of reaching the lakes are mentioned in the last paragraph, but the one described here is the classic approach, via O'Neil Pass, on one of the most spectacular trails in the national park, traversing ridges high above the Enchanted Valley of the Quinault, with many and magnificent views and flower fields.

Hike the Quinault Valley Trail 13 miles to the Enchanted Valley Chalet (Hike 95) and continue up the trail another 3½ miles to a junction, 16½ miles from the road, elevation 3300 feet.

Go right on the O'Neil Pass Trail beside a small torrent, and head westward and up, in a few yards passing a small camp. The way alternates between forest and wide-views meadows. At 1 mile are campsites and a crossing of White Creek; a hillside beyond gives the best look at Mt. Anderson.

At 1½ miles is a mountain hemlock with a sign saying it is 6 feet, 3 inches in diameter and 136 feet tall—a midget compared with the lowland species of hemlock but huge for this species. At 2 miles is an Alaska

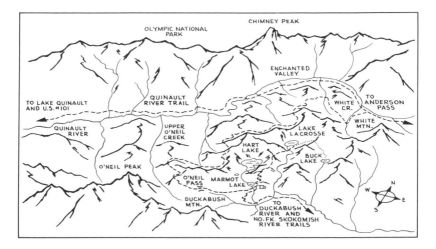

Lake LaCrosse

cedar identified as 7 feet, 6 inches in diameter and 114 feet tall.

The trail climbs to 4500 feet and then contours for miles, mainly in grass and blossoms. Directly across the valley is Chimney Peak, an impressive 6911 feet high. Views are breathtaking down the Quinault River to Lake Quinault and, if lucky, the ocean. The trail drops a bit, rounds a shoulder of the ridge, and ascends to O'Neil Pass, 7½ miles from the river, 25 miles from the road, 4900 feet, and close-ups of Mt. Duckabush. Still in meadows, the way descends to Marmot Lake, 8½ miles, 4400 feet. The O'Neil Pass Trail ends here in a junction with the Duckabush River Trail (Hike 72).

Scattered through higher gardens are Hart Lake and Lake LaCrosse. To get there, find the trail at Marmot Lake and switchback upward ¾ mile to a junction. The left fork contours ½ mile to Hart Lake, enclosed on three sides by vertical cliffs. The right fork continues ¾ mile uphill to Lake LaCrosse, 4800 feet, perhaps the most splendid alpine lake in the Olympics, with views across the water to massive 6233-foot Mt. Duckabush and more graceful 6300-foot Mt. Steel. An experienced hiker can find more private meadows and lakes.

The camping is stove-only, no wood fires, at Marmot, Hart, and LaCrosse Lakes and O'Neil Pass. Best and most crowded is the south side of Marmot Lake.

The lakes can be approached in various other ways. For one, hike the Dosewallips Trail (Hike 75) and drop over Anderson Pass 1½ miles, losing 1100 feet, to the start of the O'Neil Pass Trail. Or, hike directly to the lakes by way of the Duckabush River Trail 20 miles to Marmot Lake, gaining 4500 feet, including some major ups and downs and one difficult river crossing. For another, hike the North Fork Skokomish River Trail (Hike 69) 19½ miles to Marmot Lake, gaining 5200 feet, counting ups and downs. The lakes can also be included in imaginative one-way and loop trips.

97 POINT OF THE ARCHES

**Round trip to Point of the Arches
7 miles
Hiking time 4 hours
High point 150 feet
Hikable all year
One day or backpack**

**Maps: Custom Correct North
Olympic Coast, Green Trails
Cape Flattery (No. 98S)
Park Service backcountry use
permit required**

Here, perhaps, is the most scenic single segment of the Washington ocean coast, with needlelike sea stacks, caves, and arches to explore, tidal pools, and miles of sand beaches. Once threatened by road-building and subdivision, in 1976 Shi-Shi Beach and the Point were added to the wilderness-ocean section of Olympic National Park.

Unfortunately, for now there is no legal trail access to Shi-Shi Beach from the Makah Reservation. Beach hiking from Cape Alava is extremely difficult, and during rainy periods and high tides, the Ozette River is impossible to ford. Finding a new route is a high priority for both the Makah Indians and the National Park Service. In the meantime, the Makahs are building a new trail in 1996 to Cape Flattery, the northern tip of Washington State.

A road is on the Makah Indian Reservation. The ocean beach and all adjacent land belong to the Makahs so private property rules apply.

The undrivable road over Portage Head is pleasant walking under a canopy of trees. During wet weather be prepared for much mud. In about 1 mile push through the roadside brush for dramatic looks down to the surf. At 2 miles, where the road comes to the edge of the bluff for the first unobstructed views of the ocean is the park boundary and permit box. A trail drops to the north end of Shi-Shi Beach. (If the tide is high, follow the "road," which dwindles to a track and in a mile nearly touches the beach.)

A short sidetrip north from the foot of the trail is the south end of Por-

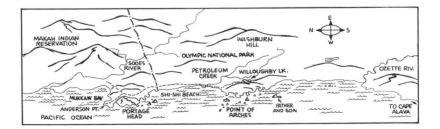

Point of the Arches

tage Head, with spectacular sea stacks, tidal pools, and whatever is left of a 1950s shipwreck. For Point of the Arches, hike about 2 miles south on the beach, leaving the reservation, passing a number of good camps (the most reliable source of water in summer is Petroleum Creek). The long string of stacks and islands can be reached and explored at very low tide; the going is rough over sharp and slippery rocks and involves some wading.

CAPE ALAVA– SAND POINT LOOP

Loop trip 9½ miles
Hiking time 6 hours
High point 170 feet
Elevation gain about 500 feet

Hikable all year
One day or backpack
Maps: Custom Correct Ozette
Beach Loop, Green Trails
Ozette (No. 130S)

Two trails from Ozette Lake to the ocean, plus the connecting stretch of Olympic National Park wilderness beach, make a magnificent loop hike for one day or several, for winter as well as summer, passing a deserted homestead, site of an Indian village, a fascinating cluster of petroglyphs, and miles of wild surf.

Drive from Port Angeles on SR 112 past Sekiu and turn left on the Ozette Lake Road to the road-end ranger station, campground, and parking lot where the Ozette River flows from the lake, elevation 36 feet. Both trails depart from the open-air information booth. The loop is equally good in either direction. The trail begins by crossing a bridge over the Ozette and in a few feet the trail splits.

If the counterclockwise loop is chosen, take the Cape Alava Trail, which goes a short bit on abandoned road and plunges into dense greenery of salal, hemlock, and other shrubs and trees. The path is sometimes flat, sometimes up and down a little, much of the way on planks—which may puzzle and irritate summertime hikers but not those who do the trip

Common murre

Pictographs near Cape Alava

in fall or spring when all the bare ground is black muck, or in winter when every depression is feet deep in water. Walk with caution—the planks can be slippery and memories of the average hiker include a pratfall or two. Lug soles are not recommended; ripple or smooth rubber soles give better traction.

At 2 miles the route opens out magically into a broad bog—Ahlstroms Prairie, partly a onetime lake filled in by natural processes, partly a pasture cleared early in the century by a homesteader, Lars Ahlstrom. Again the trail enters greenery, a far-off roar can be heard, the way tops a forested crest—and below are the loud breakers and beyond is the Pacific horizon. The trail quickly drops to the beach of Cape Alava, 3½ miles.

Camping space for scores of people (but often overcrowded in summer by hundreds of people) is available on a grassy wave-cut bench, the site of an Indian village occupied for centuries. There are many, many ghosts here; archaeologists have excavated houses buried in a mudslide 500 years ago; other buried houses, dating back at least 2500 years, are awaiting excavation. Artifacts are on display in the Makah Museum in Neah Bay. For a sidetrip, hike 1½ miles north to the Ozette River and a far look toward Point of the Arches (Hike 97).

The beach south 3 miles to Sand Point is easy walking at anything less than high tide and offers an assortment of sands and rocks and tidal pools; camps and dependable water at several places. A third of the way south, 1 mile, is Wedding Rock, inscribed with easy-to-miss petroglyphs. A dozen or more are scattered over rocks near the line of high tide.

In trees along the beach south of Sand Point are countless good (and in summer, crowded) camping areas. For sidetrips south, see Hike 99.

To complete the loop, find the trail in the woods at Sand Point and hike 3 miles to Ozette Lake, again on planks in lush brush and forest.

99 RIALTO BEACH–CAPE ALAVA– OZETTE LAKE

One-way trip 23 miles
Allow 3 days
High point 100 feet
Hikable all year

Maps: Custom Correct North
Olympic Coast, Green Trails
Ozette (No. 130S)
Park Service backcountry use
permit required

Olympic National Park first became famous for rainforests and glaciers set within a magnificently large area of mountain wilderness. Now, though, it is known far and wide for still another glory—the last long stretch of wilderness ocean beach remaining in the conterminous United States. North and south from the Quillayute River extend miles and miles of coastline that are now almost exactly as they were before Columbus—except that in 1492 (and until fairly recent times) Indians had permanent homes and temporary camps at many places along the coast now deserted.

Winter and early spring often offer the best hiking weather of the year, but storms can be hazardous. Facing a cold rain with miles of beach to hike is miserable and can lead to hypothermia.

The north section, from Rialto Beach to Cape Alava, is a longer but easier walk than the south section described in Hike 100. There are no really difficult creek crossings, only one headland that cannot be rounded at low tide, and the way mainly is simple sand and shingle, interrupted by stretches of cobbles and rough boulders.

Be sure to obtain a tide chart beforehand and use it to plan each day's schedule. Much of the route can be traveled at high tide but at the cost of scrambling over driftwood and slippery rocks, plodding wearily through steep, loose cobbles and gravel, and climbing up and down points. Moreover, some headlands cannot be climbed over and the beach at low tide provides the only passage. Be prepared to hike early in the morning or late in the evening, with layovers during the day, if the tides so dictate.

Also beforehand, pick up the Park Service brochure "Olympic Coastal Strip," which will add immeasurably to your enjoyment by explaining what you see and by helping plan a safe and pleasant trip.

Drive US 101 to 2 miles north of Forks. Turn west on the LaPush Road 8 miles, then turn right on the Mora Campground–Rialto Beach Road 5 miles to the parking lot at the beach and head north.

In ½ mile is Ellen Creek, the first permissible campsite. Here and elsewhere the "ocean tea," the creek's water colored by bark tannin dissolved in headwater swamps, is perfectly drinkable when treated as you would any other water found in the wilds. At 1½ miles, walk through the Hole in the Wall to the first headland, which has several small points, one requiring low tide to get around. At 2½ miles are camps near the Chilean Memorial, which commemorates one of the countless ships wrecked on this rugged coast, and at 3 miles begins the long, rough rounding of Cape Johnson, which has no trail over the top and can be passed at low tide

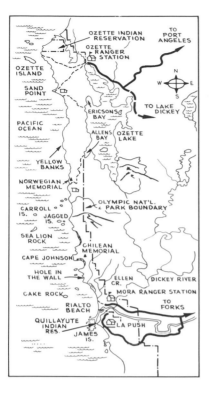

Beach near Hole in the Wall

only, as is true of another rough point immediately following. A point at 5 miles must be climbed over on a short trail and one at 6 miles rounded at low tide. At 6½ miles is Cedar Creek (campsites) and immediately beyond is a point that can be rounded at low tide or crossed on a steep, short path.

At the Norwegian Memorial (another shipwreck and more camps), 7½ miles, a rough, abandoned trail leads inland 2¼ miles to Allens Bay on Ozette Lake. (There is no trail along the lake, so this is not a shortcut to civilization.) Passing campsites every so often and at 10 miles a low-tide-only point, at 13½ miles the way comes to Yellow Banks; the point at the north end must be rounded at low tide.

At 15 miles a way trail heads inland 2 miles to Ericsons Bay on Ozette Lake. At Sand Point, 15½ miles, are innumerable campsites in the woods and a trail leading 3 miles to the Ozette Lake Road.

Don't stop here. Continue on the wilderness beach 3 miles to Cape Alava, 18½ miles (Hike 98) and finish the trip by following the trail 3½ miles back to Ozette Lake for a total of 23 miles.

THIRD BEACH
TO HOH RIVER

One-way trip 17 miles
Allow 3 days
High point 250 feet
Hikable all year
Day hike or backpack

Maps: Custom Correct South
Olympic Coast, Green Trails La
Push (No. 163S)
Park Service backcountry use
permit required

Wild forest and wild ocean, woods animals and sea birds, tidal pools and wave-carved stacks, the constant thunder of surf, and always the vast, mysterious horizon of the Pacific. This south section of the Olympic National Park wilderness ocean strip is shorter but more complicated than the northern one described in Hike 99, requiring detours inland to cross headlands and creeks and demanding even closer attention to the tide chart.

In moving toward minimal impact, the National Park Service says: "No pets, camp on the beach when tides allow, bury human waste in forested areas well back from the beach, streams, trails and campsites. Dismantle any driftwood shelters or furniture you construct; build campfires in scooped out depression in the sand when possible."

Warning: Goodman, Falls, and Mosquito Creeks are high all winter and after periods of heavy rain are virtually unfordable.

Drive US 101 to 2 miles north of Forks. Turn west on the La Push Road 12 miles to the parking lot at the Third Beach Trail, elevation 240 feet.

Warning: Cars at the Third Beach parking area are occasionally broken into. Do not leave any valuables inside the car.

Hike the forest trail, descending abruptly to the beach and campsites at 1½ miles. Head south along the sand and in ½ mile look for a prominent marker on a tree above the beach, the start of the trail over Taylor Point—which cannot be rounded at the base. The trail climbs into lovely woods, dropping back to the beach in another 1¼ miles beside a small head that can be rounded at a medium tide or climbed over on a steep path.

At 3½ miles is a point that can be rounded at low tide or climbed over by a short trail to reach Scott Creek, with campsites in the woods; another very small point immediately south can be rounded in medium tide or climbed over. At 5 miles is Strawberry Point, low and forested and

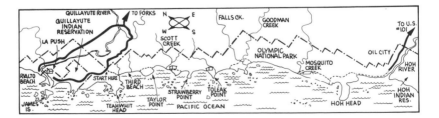

Toleak Point

simple, and at 6½ miles, Toleak Point, ditto. Shortly beyond is Jackson Creek (camps).

At 7 miles a trail ascends a steep bluff and proceeds inland through beautiful forest to crossings of Falls and Goodman Creeks (cliffs rule out a shore passage), returning to the surf at 8¾ miles. The beach is then easy to Mosquito Creek, 11 miles; ford the stream at low tide. Camps here. There now is a choice of routes. On a *minus tide in calm weather* follow the beach, crossing four or five small points; less exciting but more certain, take the overland trail.

At 13½ miles a trail climbs the large promontory of Hoh Head, which cannot be rounded in any tide, and regains the beach at 14½ miles. Going by a campsite or two, at 15 miles the way comes to the last point, a heap of big rocks that must be rounded at low tide. From here a narrow, low-tide-only strip of beach leads to the mouth of the Hoh River, 16 miles. A trail follows the river inland to the Oil City road-end, 17 miles. To find the Oil City Road drive US 101 about 0.5 mile north of the Hoh River bridge and go west on the road signed "Cottonwood Recreation Area" 12 miles to the road-end.

INDEX

THE MOUNTAINEERS, founded in 1906, is a non-profit outdoor activity and conservation club, whose mission is "to explore, study, preserve and enjoy the natural beauty of the outdoors..." Based in Seattle, Washington, the club is now the third largest such organization in the United States, with 12,000 members and four branches throughout Washington State.

The Mountaineers sponsors both classes and year-round outdoor activities in the Pacific Northwest, which include hiking, mountain climbing, ski-touring, snowshoeing, bicycling, camping, kayaking and canoeing, nature study, sailing, and adventure travel. The club's conservation division supports environmental causes through educational activities, sponsoring legislation, and presenting informational programs. All club activities are led by skilled, experienced volunteers, who are dedicated to promoting safe and responsible enjoyment and preservation of the outdoors.

The Mountaineers Books, an active, non-profit publishing program of the club, produces guidebooks, instructional texts, historical works, natural history guides, and works on environmental conservation. All books produced by the Mountaineers are aimed at fulfilling the club's mission.

If you would like to participate in these organized outdoor activities or the club's programs, consider a membership in The Mountaineers. For information and an application, write or call The Mountaineers, Club Headquarters, 300 Third Avenue West, Seattle, Washington 98119; (206) 284-6310.